hamlyn | **all colour petcare**

dog tricks

KT-364-371

Over 50 fun tricks to teach your dog

Mary Ray
Justine Harding

hamlyn

An Hachette UK Company
www.hachette.co.uk

First published in Great Britain in 2009 by Hamlyn,
a division of Octopus Publishing Group Ltd
2–4 Heron Quays, London E14 4JP
www.octopusbooks.co.uk

ISBN 978 0 600 61827 0

A CIP catalogue record for this book is available from
the British Library.

Printed and bound in China.

10 9 8 7 6 5 4 3 2 1

Note Unless the information is specific to males or
females, throughout this book puppies and dogs are
referred to as 'he' and the information and advice are
applicable to both sexes.

No dogs or puppies were harmed in the making of
this book.

DogsTrust

Dogs Trust is the UK's largest dog welfare charity
and campaigns on dog welfare issues to ensure
a safe and happy future for all dogs. The charity
has a network of 17 centres across the UK and
cares for over 16,000 stray and abandoned dogs
each year. The charity is well known for its
slogan 'A Dog Is For Life, Not Just For Christmas'
and is working towards the day when all dogs
can enjoy a happy life, free from the threat of
unnecessary destruction.

If you are interested in rehoming a dog
you can visit the Dogs Trust website at
www.dogstrust.org.uk and click on Rehoming,
or call **020 7837 0006** to find your nearest centre.

Registered charity numbers 227523 and SC037843

hamlyn | **all colour petcare**

dog tricks

Contents

Why teach tricks?

Teaching your dog tricks is rewarding, entertaining and gives you the chance to show others just how smart your dog is. Your dog will benefit physically and mentally, and the pair of you build a better relationship. Your understanding of one another improves, along with the trust between you. In short, you and your dog will enjoy each other's company more.

Tricks are simply an extension of the training that responsible owners already do with their pets. They just take your dog's skills to a higher level. If you watch dogs playing together, you will see them naturally performing many of the moves that are taught to be performed on cue in this book. When dogs are kept

An educated and stimulated dog is a happy one.

alone, these behaviours tend to be lost, but they can be triggered again with training.

What's in it for your dog?

- Quality time with you

- A chance to really use his brain

- Improvement in physical fitness and suppleness

- Lots of fun and treats

- A happy owner

What's in it for you?

- Quality time with your dog

- The reward of seeing your dog's enjoyment at showing off his talents

- The surprise of learning just how smart your dog is

- Lots of fun

- A more responsive, obedient, happy dog

Praise, not punishment

Tricks were once seen as bad things to teach to animals – not because of the tricks themselves, but because of the way they were taught. The modern training methods taught in this book mean that punishment is never used, only rewards and praise. Plus, good trainers learn to make the most out of the behaviours that each individual dog naturally shows. It is not surprising then that, by using this approach, dogs thoroughly enjoy learning new tricks and are eager to show what they can do in the hope of getting another treat.

Dog-owning is all about building a rewarding relationship for you both.

Dogs are very intelligent and need to have their minds occupied, but too often they are not challenged enough and will find their own ways to stimulate their brains. This is when behavioural problems can arise due to boredom and frustration. By teaching tricks, you can give your dog plenty to think about and so help prevent these issues from developing – or even help solve those that are already there. As the saying goes, the dog is man's best friend, but if he is taught

some basic skills and tricks, he will become an even better friend.

Of course, you don't get all these benefits without some investment. Spending just five minutes each day with your dog (and longer sessions when you can) will be enough to see great results. If you have any hiccups along the way, simply refer to the 'training checklist' on page 25 to help overcome any minor difficulties before they become bigger problems that will be harder to resolve.

Assess for success

So you and your dog are keen to start learning some smart moves. You may even already have your eye on a few tricks that you feel are particularly impressive. That's great – with that enthusiasm you'll go far. However, your particular dog should also have an influence on the tricks you choose and how you teach them.

Early training will be through play and develops as your puppy matures.

Dogs come in all shapes, sizes, types, breeds, ages and abilities. While nearly all are capable of learning tricks, your training will be much more successful if you take these characteristics into account from the outset.

Age

Contrary to the adage that you can't teach an old dog new tricks, in fact, no dog is too old to learn new tricks. Consider what training he has done already, as well as his fitness and health. For example, a dog that is stiff in his hips and has had only limited training won't achieve reversing backwards (see page 130) as easily as giving a paw (see page 54). Equally, young dogs and puppies will not be physically or mentally mature enough for some moves, especially those involving jumping or being in an upright position. Instead, concentrate on

other tricks for now and build up from there to the more demanding tricks.

Type or breed

Your dog's type will also affect which tricks he excels at and which he finds harder. For example, small dogs usually find upright tricks like standing on their hindlegs very easy. But there are always exceptions to the rule. One particular 12-year-old Bulldog, for instance, easily does high fives (see page 64) and creeps backwards, despite his natural shape suggesting that he would find both of these actions hard to do.

Border Collies are often thought of as the crème de la crème of dogs for specialist training due to their intelligence and willingness to please. But although they are very clever, being an 'eye' breed, Collies like to be actually shown what is required. Other breeds or crossbreeds are often better at thinking for themselves. So whatever your dog's shape, breed or type, have a go – you'll probably be surprised at what you can both achieve with a bit of work.

Where to train your dog

You can easily teach your dog tricks at home and in your garden, and as you and he get more confident, practise out on walks. At home your dog should be relaxed and confident and so ready to learn. Always choose a room with a non-slip, soft floor, such as carpet, so that your dog feels that he has a good footing and is comfortable if you ask him to lie down. Make sure you have plenty of clear floor space so that your dog can move around confidently, without colliding with furniture, and can easily find treats thrown to him. Choose quiet, confined spaces to begin with to help your dog keep focused on you. As he improves, practise your tricks where there are distractions.

Left- or right-pawed?

Just like humans, dogs tend to be right- or left-handed, so will find some tricks easier to do on one side than the other. Watch how your dog moves and see which side he naturally favours. By knowing if your dog is right- or left-handed, you can then help him to learn new things more easily by always starting on his 'easier' side. Also, by teaching him tricks on both sides, he will become more balanced and supple.

Keep playtime and lessons separate initially, to save frustration for you both.

What you need

To do any job well, you need the right tools, and dog training is no exception. You are likely to have quite a few of the things you'll need already, while others you won't need until you start to do the more advanced tricks.

Collar and lead

You will require a lead only if your dog initially has to work on his basic training (see page 26). Most tricks are best taught off lead. Choose a full leather collar of a thickness to suit your dog's neck and adjust it so that you can just fit two fingers under it. The lead needs to sit in your hand comfortably, and be thick and long enough for the size of your dog, but not so long that you cannot easily take up the slack.

Dog toys

You probably already have a selection of dog toys and a good idea of what your dog likes. Tug toys are good for training, as long as your dog enjoys them, as you can play with him but still get the toy back readily. Keep a couple of favourite toys for training sessions only.

Dog toys

Collar and lead

Treats

Target stick

Clickers

Treats

Choose a mix of high-value treats that your dog loves. Usually cooked meat, cheese or frankfurters are the most prized. Find out more about choosing and using treats on page 14.

Treat bag or pot

A bag that fits round your waist is ideal. You can get treats for your dog easily, wherever you are, while keeping your hands free. Alternatively, have a full treat pot near by.

Clicker

This is a small, hand-held device that has a metal tongue that emits a 'click-click' sound when pressed. It is used to tell your dog when he has done the right thing (see page 18). A box clicker has the tongue set within it and is operated with your thumb, while the button clicker has a push button, so can be operated under your foot.

Puppy pen

Puppy pen

This is a multi-panelled, hinged wire fence that can be arranged in a number of different shapes. Although designed for keeping puppies out of mischief, it is ideal for teaching certain more advanced tricks, too. However, you can also improvise with what you may have available.

Target markers and sticks

Some tricks can be taught more effectively using a 'target', which gives the dog a clear point to touch or follow. A target marker is a small mat, plastic lid or flat piece of wood usually used to position a dog (see pages 157 and 160). A target stick, like the one pictured on page 11, is an extendable wand. With the aid of different 'attachments' on the end, such as a small ball or a flat, rectangular piece of plastic or wood (see pages 157 and 158), you can teach your dog to move in new ways.

Basket

Ball

Poles and jumps

If you want to teach weaving, pole-related tricks or jumping, you'll need these. You can buy specially designed poles and cone bases from suppliers of equipment for agility, which have a dual purpose – the poles can stand upright in a cone base for weaving or be laid horizontally across two cones to form jumps. You can make your own poles for weaving from a lightweight broom handle set into a heavy block, so that it cannot easily be knocked over. In contrast, when making your own jumps, you need to use something that can easily be knocked down without causing any discomfort to your dog, such as a bamboo cane.

Props

In the book, a hoop, cane, basket, skateboard, blanket, ball and wastebin are used, but you can adapt the tricks to suit what you have to hand. Let your imagination run wild!

Poles and cones

Teaching tricks using food

Most dogs love food and will do almost anything to get it! Even dogs who aren't bothered about treats will become keener once 'high-value' foods are used. Just like us, dogs will only work if their 'pay' is worth it.

For training, 'real' food is the best, as it is very desirable to your dog. Always use food that doesn't crumble and is visible if thrown to the floor, and cut it into thumbnail-sized cubes. Give any food the three-second test: can your dog – and does he want to – chew and swallow it in under three seconds? If not, it will have no value in training.

With food held in your fingertips, you can 'lure' your dog in any direction.

To maximize the effectiveness of your treats, make sure your dog hasn't just eaten before training. However, he shouldn't be 'starving' as this can turn eagerness for treats into frustration, or worse, aggression.

Using food to train

Food is used in two ways to teach your dog tricks. First, it is a reward – give the treat as soon as your dog does as you have asked, either directly from your hand or by throwing it to him. By throwing treats, you can reward him more quickly when he is at a distance from you and prevent your dog anticipating food always coming from your hand.

Second, food can be used to show your dog what you want – this is called luring. By holding a tasty treat in the tips of your fingers close to his nose, you can encourage him to follow your hand into the position or through the move you are teaching. Experiment with how your hand position affects your dog's movement. The position

Key points

● Luring requires your dog to watch the food, rather than to grab at it. Teach your dog not to snatch by holding the treat firmly between the tips of your fingers, so that he can smell it but not actually get it. Keep your hand still and wait until he stops biting at the treat. As soon as he pulls back slightly, give it to him. By repeating this, you will soon teach your dog that he gets the food more easily by being patient.

● Take care not to drop crumbs on the floor, as your dog will soon learn to look for 'freebies' rather than at you.

● Make sure you are always the best source of food around, then your dog will have no need to look anywhere else for treats.

of his nose will determine the direction of the rest of his body. For example, if you encourage him to lift his nose high, his tail is likely to go down, so this will help you to ask him to sit. To help lure your dog successfully, practise both the overhand position and the underhand position shown above.

While luring can be used as a training method in itself, it is more effective when used alongside clicker training (see page 18).

Overhand

Underhand

The right rewards

Many owners find that their dog will work for them only if they have food. Dogs are often given little reward or have their reward cut out too quickly after learning something new. Be generous with your treats, especially early on in training, so that your dog knows his effort is worthwhile. As he begins to understand and enjoy the trick, start reducing the rewards, offer them more randomly or ask for more work in return.

Canine communication

Dogs are masters of body language, but sadly we humans are not. Owners are often convinced that they are telling their dog to do one thing, usually with their voice, but, in fact, their body position is saying the complete opposite.

To train your dog successfully, you need to tell him clearly and consistently what you want – the better at this you are, the quicker and easier he will learn. As well as using your voice and body language, communicate with him using facial expressions, touch, hand signals and, as you'll see throughout this book, the clicker (see page 18).

What barking means

Barking is frequently the response of a confused or frustrated dog. This is your dog asking for more clues as to what you want. Don't keep trying the same thing, but go back to the last step he understood. Then give him some further pointers to what you want now, checking that your signals are clear.

Always use the hand closest to your dog to lure or signal, to avoid confusion.

Body language

Dogs tune into your silhouette, so aim to keep your body shape clear. Always use the hand on the side closest to your dog to lure or signal, rather than crossing your arms over your body. Often, your dog may not read the signal you think you are giving him, but takes his cue from something more subtle. Be aware of how your movement can affect your dog's – stepping into him will make him hesitant to come close to you again. Leaning over your dog can be threatening, especially for small dogs or puppies, so try kneeling down. Always allow your dog enough room to complete the move you are asking for.

Hand signals

When teaching a trick, start with large movements and gradually reduce them. This makes the signals clear and easier for your dog to follow. If using hand signals to cue your dog for a trick, they need to be distinct.

Voice

Think carefully about verbal commands to avoid confusing your dog. Words can sound similar, such as 'bow' and 'down'. Vary the tone of your commands – use a higher-pitched voice for upwards moves and lower tones for downward moves.

Key points

● A dog can perform a trick from a voice, hand or body signal.

● The movement you use initially to lure your dog will form the first visual cue.

● When the dog can do the trick following just your hand movement, add the verbal command you wish to use.

● Use verbal and visual cues together, so that your dog connects both to the trick.

● With practice, your dog will perform from just a voice command or just a visual signal.

Use big signals when teaching a trick before refining them to near invisible cues.

Introducing the clicker

If you are familiar with the traditional methods of dog training, prepare yourself for a new astonishing, rewarding and fun experience: clicker training.

And don't be tempted to disregard it as a gimmick – even some highly sceptical professionals have been won round to the clicker approach after seeing what it can achieve. The method was originally developed by dolphin trainer Karen Pryor and it has since taken dog training on in leaps and bounds. But why is it so good? The five main reasons are:

1 Your dog quickly learns that each time he hears a click he will always gets a reward.
2 You can mark the exact behaviour you want your dog to repeat with a click.
3 The click remains consistent, so it is easy for your dog to understand.
4 The clicker provides a bridge between your dog's behaviour and the reward, as you can tell him he has done well even if you cannot

Clicker training can boost a dog's confidence as well as his repertoire of skills.

The clicker

Box clickers are the most common (see page 11) and
work simply by pressing down the metal tongue in
the centre with your thumb and releasing, which
produces a 'click-click'. Always aim to hold the clicker
in the hand away from your dog, with food treats in the
hand closest to him. Avoid clicking close to your dog's ear.

give him a treat instantly. A click promises a
reward. This is invaluable especially when
your dog is at a distance from you or in the
middle of a move that you don't want to
interrupt with a treat.

5 Your dog is encouraged to think and work
out for himself what you want – rather than
just being taught parrot-fashion – so he will
actively participate in and enjoy his lessons.

Clicker training is all about letting your dog
use his own brain and be part of the training
process – this is what makes it so enjoyable.
There is no punishment, just the opportunity
to try again, or praise for doing the right
thing, which creates confidence. Even the
quietest, most retiring dogs that are normally
far too shy to do anything in front of other
people can become confident, responsive
trick artists with clicker training – and the

Sheltie pictured left is one such example,
being transformed from the most reluctant
performer to a dog willing to take part in
dog-training demonstrations at Crufts.

Clicking for tricks

All the tricks in this book follow this same basic training sequence, which, once you and your dog have tuned into it, will get progressively easier.

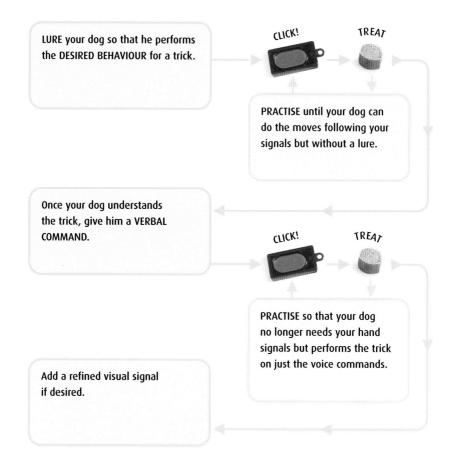

LURE your dog so that he performs the DESIRED BEHAVIOUR for a trick.

CLICK!

TREAT

PRACTISE until your dog can do the moves following your signals but without a lure.

Once your dog understands the trick, give him a VERBAL COMMAND.

CLICK!

TREAT

PRACTISE so that your dog no longer needs your hand signals but performs the trick on just the voice commands.

Add a refined visual signal if desired.

Selective clicking

Once your dog understands that 'click' always means reward, you have a vast array of possibilities at your fingertips. For example, the clicker can be used to 'capture' natural behaviours, such as a leg stretch or a head shake. Simply wait for the behaviour to occur, click and treat, and your dog will quickly try to re-create what resulted in the reward. However, be aware that any behaviour occurring as you click may be reproduced by your dog. So, if you click him for wagging his tail but he barks at the same time, you may inadvertently encourage him to bark. Unwanted behaviours can simply be taken back out of your dog's repertoire by never clicking them again.

While food is best for training many dogs, others just love their toys.

Key points

● As you start to use the clicker, don't feel that you need to use your voice as well – the click will praise your dog. Even verbal commands are introduced later, the idea being that only the full move in its finished form is associated with the command you are going to use.

● A click always promises a reward – the majority of dogs work well for food, but time playing with a toy or a pat and a cuddle can be used, too.

Clicking for tricks

So now you know what a clicker is and what it can offer. Better still, your enthusiasm for it is likely to grow as you see the results for yourself. First, however, your dog has to learn that the clicker is significant for him, too. At the moment, a clicking sound will not mean much to him. You need to teach him that the click is positive, rewarding and well worth responding to. From this simple but crucial lesson, the rest of your dog's training will begin to fall into place.

1 Call your dog to you and give him a few treats so that he knows you have them.

2 Hold the clicker in one hand and a treat in the other. Simply click and immediately afterwards give your dog a treat. Keep repeating this, clicking when your dog is looking at you – soon your dog will get excited each time he hears a click and watch you for the next treat.

3 You can then try throwing a piece of food on the floor. Click just before your dog eats it and then repeat.

4 Now test that your dog understands that clicks equal rewards. Choose a simple command that he already knows, such as 'sit'. Command 'sit', making a click as he does this, and reward once he's sitting. Then move away a few steps – he is likely to follow you for more treats. Again tell him to 'sit', click as he reaches a sit and reward. Move away once more, but this time say nothing – he should come and sit beside you of his own accord. Just click and treat.

Training checklist

As you try the tricks in this book, there will be times when things don't go quite according to plan. If ever there's a hiccup, take a minute to read this checklist – the chances are that it will get you back on the road to success.

☑ A click ALWAYS gets at least one reward.

☑ Click as soon as your dog begins doing the move you want, then reward.

☑ Only use high-value treats and plenty of them (see page 14).

☑ Only click once at any one time, even if you give lots of treats.

☑ Give your dog time to work out for himself what is required.

☑ Build up gradually – at the start of a new trick, click for small steps towards the end goal. For example, to get your dog to twist, you may begin by clicking for just a turn of his head, where he could turn a full circle for a click once he's got the idea.

☑ Keep your dog guessing – about when and how many treats he will get. Although rewards must always be worthwhile, sometimes give a handful for doing particularly well and occasionally ask for two or three repetitions of a move before rewarding.

☑ Don't always click at the end of a behaviour, as this will teach your dog to always stop dead at this point. For example, on circle moves, sometimes click after half a revolution, sometimes after one-and-a-half circles.

☑ You get what you click, so make sure your timing is right.

☑ Experiment! The clicker is very versatile and its advantages are best discovered through trying different things. You can do little harm and any undesirable behaviours that you accidentally train in your dog can usually be just as easily untrained.

Walk this way

When your dog pulls tight on his lead, you are off balance and out of control. Most tricks are best taught with your dog off lead, so he needs to learn to stay close to you and pay attention. A dog that is constantly pulling and looking the other way isn't going to learn much. This simple exercise will show your dog that it is much more rewarding to stay close to you and that hauling on his lead only results in neck ache.

1 When your dog pulls, stop and plant yourself to the floor. Stay where you are and wait for him to stop or turn towards you. As soon as the lead goes slack, click.

2 Immediately walk forwards to meet your dog, so that you come together again with him on your left side.

3 Once you are side by side with your dog on a loose lead, give him a treat. Repeat the exercise several times – your dog will soon hang back beside your leg in anticipation of another reward.

4 As your dog gets the idea, begin working him in a large circle. At this stage, always have him on the outside of the circle, whether he is on your left or right – he will find it easier to achieve a flowing movement. Walk at a brisk pace for three or four strides, and if he is still on a loose lead and focused on you, click, then stop and reward him. Get his attention back onto your hand before setting off again to repeat the process.

Key points

● Avoid letting your lead hang too low when your dog is walking well, so it cannot trip up either of you.

● Working your dog on the outside of a circle will encourage him to watch you, as you are in effect always turning and walking away from him.

● With particularly strong dogs, hold the lead with both hands so that it comes from your dog, through your left hand, then diagonally across your body into your right hand. This will give you more control should your dog suddenly pull.

Loose-lead therapy

How a dog walks on his lead can affect how he reacts to different situations. A tight lead may give a bold, aggressive dog more confidence, however this type of dog is often unassertive on a loose lead. A tight lead can also make a nervous dog more worried, as he feels his option to take flight from anything that may concern him is taken away. With these dogs, a loose lead will make them more confident.

Total recall

There is little point in having a dog who can perform spectacular tricks if you can't get him to come to you when you want. In order to train him and keep him safe, you need to be able to call your dog to you instantly. For him to leave the exciting things he's just found, your dog needs to be convinced that there's something in it for him.

1 When your dog is a little way from you, call him by name to get his attention. You can rustle the treats to get him to look towards you. As soon as he turns to face you, click.

2 Your dog should already understand that a click means a treat, so he'll come to you to get his reward. It really is as easy as that.

Key points

● Call your dog's name only once, so that it maintains impact. Make your voice exciting, backed up with treats or a toy to ensure that you get a reaction. He will quickly 'tune out' your voice if you keep shouting but nothing else interesting happens.

● Many dogs won't return to their owners because they are punished when they do finally go back. This just teaches the dog that going to that person is unpleasant.

● Another common cause of a dog not recalling is the owner chasing after him. A dog will think you are playing a game. If it is safe to do so, get your dog's attention and then run away – he is likely to follow quickly.

3 As soon as he comes to you, reward him. If he's reluctant to come in close, crouch down or even step backwards. With the task complete, walk away a short distance before recalling him. Once your dog comes to you quickly and reliably as soon as you call, introduce the command 'come'. Call his name, command him and, as he comes towards you, click. Treat as soon as he reaches you.

Early learning

Teaching a dog to stay or come back should begin in puppyhood, as this is the time that dogs are most likely to stick with their human 'pack'. Choose safe, secure places and walk away from your pup as he watches. His curiosity and need for reassurance will soon get the better of him.

Take a seat

To perform tricks, your dog needs to be agile and able to move between different positions easily, especially if you want him to do a sequence of moves. The basis of many tricks will be a sit, so as well as doing this on command, he needs to be able to move into sit from whatever he was doing before. Teaching your dog to sit from any position is all about positioning his nose correctly, as this will influence how he moves his hindquarters. If your dog's nose is held high, it is physically easier for him to keep his hindquarters low.

1 Hold a treat in the underhand position (see page 15) at your dog's nose level and call your dog so that he is standing in front of you at arm's length.

Sitting styles

Did you know that from a standing position dogs can sit in two different ways? Those favouring a 'forwards' sit keep their front legs still and bring their hindlegs under them to meet their front paws. Big breeds and those with a 'stiff-legged' gait, such as Dobermans, Standard Poodles and larger terrier breeds, tend to 'backwards' sit. Keeping their hind feet planted, they draw their front feet back to their hind feet and simply hinge backwards into a sit.

2 In one smooth, steady movement, rotate your hand to the overhand position (see page 15) and raise it straight above your dog's nose, before pushing it out towards your dog's tail. His nose will follow upwards and then tip back slightly, making it easier for him to drop his hindquarters. As soon as he moves into a sit, click. Once he is sitting, give him his reward. Repeat until your dog understands the move, then add in the 'sit' command just before you click.

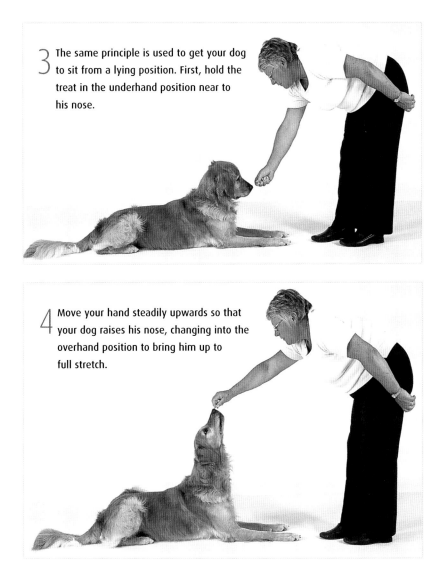

3 The same principle is used to get your dog to sit from a lying position. First, hold the treat in the underhand position near to his nose.

4 Move your hand steadily upwards so that your dog raises his nose, changing into the overhand position to bring him up to full stretch.

5 Now push your hand steadily upwards and backwards so that, to follow the treat, your dog has to push himself upwards and step backwards with his front legs into a sit. Click just before he reaches the sitting position and reward him once he's there.

Key points

● As you move your dog from a down to a sit, make sure he doesn't stand first before sitting. You are aiming for him to hinge upwards in one, smooth move.

● When teaching your dog to sit from a down position, stand up rather than crouch.

● When asked to sit from standing, small dogs often find walking backwards easier. To overcome this habit, break the move down, clicking first for just a slight lift of the nose, again when the head tips back, then again when the hindquarters drop a little, and so on. You can also position your dog where there is a wall behind him, so that backward movement when sitting is limited.

Stand and deliver

Many tricks involving backward movement or standing on the hindlegs require your dog to be able to move easily into the standing position. For a dog to walk backwards or upright, bow and many other things, he needs to be strong in his hindlegs and confident about positioning them. As you teach your dog to stand promptly on command, aim to get him pushing himself up smartly with his hindlegs, rather than pulling himself into position with his front legs.

Stand from sit

1 To teach your dog to stand from sitting, begin with a treat held in the underhand position (see page 15) level with his nose.

2 Take one step backwards, keeping the treat at nose height and drawing your dog towards you. If your hand goes too high, your dog will return to sitting even if he has begun to stand; too low and he'll lie down.

3 As your dog squares up into a stand, click and then treat. Practise this until your dog gets the idea and then add in the command 'stand' just before you click.

Stand from down

1 From the down position, move your dog into a standing position by first holding a treat in the underhand position (see page 15) near his nose.

2 As before, take a step backwards, but this time move your hand diagonally upwards to bring your dog's nose up. His hindlegs will follow, and as he reaches standing, click and treat. Again, as he begins to get the idea add the command 'stand' just before you click.

Key points

● Make your 'stand' command distinct from the 'sit' and 'down' commands by using a different tone of voice for each – ask your dog to stand, tell him to sit and command him to lie down.

● The pitch of your voice should reflect the position you want from him – a high pitch is best for the stand, a middle pitch for sitting and a low tone for down.

Hindleg help

If dogs can judge the position of their hindquarters and place their hindlegs precisely, they will then move equally fluently at both ends of their body. One way to teach them to do this is to get them to move into a stand by 'snapping up' with their hindlegs. When your dog is lying or sitting, bring his food bowl to him and put it on the floor right under his chin, between his front legs. He will then 'flick' his hindlegs up and move into a stand to be able to reach it.

Down time

To do tricks such as roll over (see page 78) or play dead (see page 82), your dog needs to go into the down position quickly and easily with a clean drop to the floor. This needs forethought, clear communication and trust to be successful as you are asking him to go into a vulnerable position.

Down from stand

1 With your dog standing, hold a treat close to his nose in the underhand position (see page 15).

2 Encourage his front end down by moving your hand as if to take it between your dog's front legs. Move the food slowly and aim to get your dog pivoting down into the bow position (see page 84).

3 Keep your hand low and still and his hindquarters should drop. When he is almost in position, click, then reward once he is down. Repeat until he does this easily. Add the verbal command 'down' and practise – he will soon drop on the verbal command alone.

Key points

● Be clear with your command – 'down' should mean the down position and nothing else.

● Think about the surface you are asking your dog to lie on. Hard surfaces can discourage some dogs, especially hairless, thin-skinned or bony breeds, such as Greyhounds and Whippets.

● If your dog tends to step forward as you try to move him into a down, click initially just for a lowering of his head. You can then work in small stages from this to getting his front end onto the floor.

Down from sit

1 From a sitting position, move your dog into the down position by luring him forwards and downwards. Aim to move his front legs only, leaving enough room for them both to come straight forwards.

2 When he cannot reach forwards any further without moving his hindlegs, move the treat down to the floor. As he sinks into a down, click and reward. Practise, then add the 'down' command.

The three downs

There are three different down positions. The 'upright' down (left) is what you are aiming for when your dog needs to move quickly between positions. When your dog is relaxed, he may lie on one hip so that his front end is still upright but his feet are to one side of his body (middle). Then there is the 'flat' down, used for roll overs (see page 78) and playing dead (see page 82), where your dog lies stretched out on one side of his body (bottom).

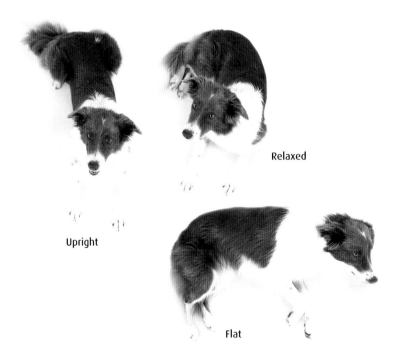

Relaxed

Upright

Flat

Hold it!

Many tricks require your dog to stay in a single position, so you need to be able to tell him to 'hold it right there'. Teach the wait command in simple positions first, such as the sit, down and stand, and once your dog understands, you can use it for begging (see page 60), playing dead (see page 82) or anything else that takes your fancy.

1 Begin by recalling your dog close to you and commanding him to 'sit'. However, instead of clicking as he sits, wait two or three seconds with him in a sit, then click and treat. Now command 'sit' again and this time don't click for five or six seconds. This will teach him to be patient for his reward and that receiving a treat does not necessarily signal the end of the exercise. Once the dog has succeeded several times, introduce the 'wait' command by saying 'sit, wait'.

Key points

● If your dog breaks from a position as you click, but before you give the treat, simply put him back where you had told him to wait and then treat. There is no need to click again, as you are still finishing the previous click/treat combination.

● The giving of the treat should not become the cue to end any exercise, especially the wait. Prevent this by giving a variable number of treats so that your dog remains focused on you in case there is more food coming.

● Use a release word such as 'OK', which indicates to your dog that the wait exercise has finished and he is now allowed to leave his spot.

● As you initially move around your dog while he waits, take care to keep your hands still and your movement controlled. Waving arms can be confusing, appearing as signals, while fast moves may look like an invitation to come and play.

2 Once your dog understands the basic idea, command him to 'sit, wait', but this time take a step away from him. If he remains sitting, click and go back to him to reward.

3 Now try linking the 'wait' command to other positions, such as the sit or stand. Give the position command first and then add 'wait'. Begin close to your dog and build up the distance.

Square standing

Make it easier for your dog to wait in the standing position by making sure he is comfortable. Teach him to stand squarely with a 'leg at each corner'. Use a treat to shuffle him forwards and backwards until he is standing with his front paws in line and back paws well under him and in line, then click and treat. Practise this so that it becomes second nature to him. Gradually he will learn to take up this stance on his own.

4 Build up the distance you can move away from him by taking another step backwards with each repetition of the exercise. Once your dog is happy for you to move away some distance, try moving from side to side. Always click when you are at the furthest point away and return to your dog to reward him.

Positions please

Teaching your dog a good heel position while walking opens up many possibilities. Moves look much slicker if you are working close together. Train your dog to position himself tightly beside your leg, with his body straight. The way your dog moves to your heel is also important. By teaching him to loop behind you to get into the heel position, he learns to step well with his hindlegs and to swing his quarters separately to his front end. This is vital for backwards moves, such as reversing around you.

1 Start with your dog facing you, slightly over to your left side. Stand with your feet together and hold a treat at nose level, close to your dog.

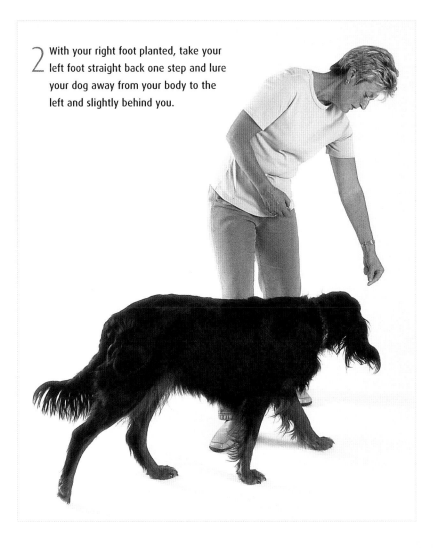

2 With your right foot planted, take your left foot straight back one step and lure your dog away from your body to the left and slightly behind you.

3 From this side position, turn your dog towards you and encourage him to move in a large anticlockwise loop behind you.

4 Make the arc big enough for your dog to turn 180 degrees so that his nose comes round just behind your left leg. You are aiming for him then to step his hindlegs to the right, to bring them in line with his head. As soon as he steps round with his hind feet, click.

Key points

● Always start this exercise with your dog in front of you, as it is then easier to make the loop correctly.

● Do not turn your dog in a loop away from your body – he should always turn towards you, reinforcing the idea that he should keep looking to you.

● Once you have practised this move a number of times and taught your dog the 'close' command, try simply holding the treat close to your leg in the position where you want his nose to end up and then giving the command. You should find that your dog will swing his hindquarters around and position himself straight and close beside you.

● Don't forget to practise this move on both sides of your body.

● Make sure you give your dog enough room to turn completely before coming back to your side.

5 Step forward with your left leg to bring your feet together and your dog forwards in line with your leg. Once he is standing close beside you with his body straight, click and give him a treat. Repeat the move by simply turning to face your dog and then following these steps again. Add the command 'close' just prior to clicking.

Shaping up

It's time to test if your dog is focusing on you and clued in fully to all you have taught him so far. Put his lead away and get active with some heelwork in different directions, on different sides of your body and in varying patterns. Wherever you go, your dog should remain in position and attentive. As well as keeping him focused, working him to heel in different ways will improve his flexibility and the strength in his hindquarters. Always start with the side he finds easiest first and keep the shapes large. As your dog becomes more supple, you can ask for tighter turns.

Circling with your dog on the outside

Practise large circles with your dog on your outside. Go clockwise when he's on your left and anticlockwise when he's on your right. Move at a brisk pace to maintain your dog's interest and momentum. Hold your treats in a position that allows your dog's head and neck to be comfortable and doesn't force his hindquarters to swing out. Circling naturally turns your dog towards you and encourages him to stride out to keep up with you.

Key points

● Always begin circle work by asking for a few good steps at heel from your dog, clicking while he is still moving well. Ask him to stop a step or two later to give him a treat.

Circling with your dog on the inside

Now try circling anticlockwise with your dog on your left and vice versa. Start with big circles so that he doesn't have to turn away from you too much. If your dog is able to work fluently on the inside of a circle, he is becoming 'back-end aware'.

Figures-of-eight

Next practise your heelwork with two circles joined to form a figure-of-eight. Your dog will need to adapt from being on the outside to the inside of the circle and back again. Try to walk the circle with your dog on the outside slightly faster than the one with him on the inside. A figure-of-eight can also help a dog who finds being on the inside tricky – you can use the straight steps as you cross over to get him back into a good heel position and rebalanced.

How do you do

This cute trick is quick and easy to teach, especially if your dog naturally uses his paws rather than his mouth to try to get hold of things. The 'give paw' command also forms the basis of other tricks, including waving (see page 56), marching (see box opposite) and high fives (see page 64). To avoid confusing your dog, use a verbal cue such as 'get it', to indicate that he can try to get the food.

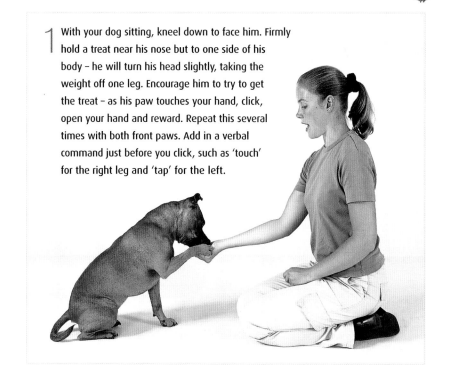

1 With your dog sitting, kneel down to face him. Firmly hold a treat near his nose but to one side of his body – he will turn his head slightly, taking the weight off one leg. Encourage him to try to get the treat – as his paw touches your hand, click, open your hand and reward. Repeat this several times with both front paws. Add in a verbal command just before you click, such as 'touch' for the right leg and 'tap' for the left.

On the march

You can make your dog march by asking for each foot in turn and slowly building up the speed. If you replace the hand signal with raising your foot (left foot then right foot) you and your dog can even march in unison!

2 With a treat in one hand, hold out your other hand in an open position towards the leg you want your dog to lift. When his paw touches your open hand, click and reward. Repeat with both front legs.

3 From an upright kneeling position, ask for his paw. He needn't actually touch your hand – click when he lifts his paw to the right position and then reward.

4 With practise you'll soon be able to get your dog to say 'how do you do' with either paw from a sit simply by showing an open hand on the side you wish him to give his paw.

Making waves

To get your dog to perform a proper wave, you simply need to refine what he does to give a paw (see page 54). The paw lift is the same – you just need to introduce movement and encourage your dog to give his paw at several different heights to produce the waving action.

1 Start by asking your dog to give his paw by holding out your hand and giving your voice command, for example 'touch' or 'tap'. Practise this several times to build up confidence and momentum.

2 This time, as your dog lifts his paw and starts to stretch towards you, move your hand up, just out of his reach. He is likely to reach out further to try to make contact with you. As his paw reaches a more extended position, click and treat. Repeat this several times, each time clicking when his paw is at a different height.

3 Gradually delay the click so that your dog has to stretch out for your hand once and then do another lower paw lift before you click and reward. Then wait for him to reach out twice before clicking and so on. Introduce the verbal command 'wave' at the end of the sequence of 'give paw' commands, for example, 'tap, tap, wave', then click and treat. As he develops a waving motion you can start to drop the command you use for giving a paw and just use 'wave'.

Key points

● Concentrate on just one front paw for this trick, with your dog in a sitting position. This will help to encourage him to produce the waving movement, rather than constantly swapping legs to try to get your hand.

● Don't ask your dog to lift his paw too high. Most dogs will be unable to lift their paw above their head without then having to slam it to the floor to regain their balance. In order to wave well, they need to be able to keep the foot off the ground.

The dog goes as if to shake hands...

...but continues to lift his paw...

...and strikes out upwards before repeating the move again to create a wave.

Shake a leg

Most dogs can quickly be taught to lift a front paw on cue, but how about a hindleg? This trick can be developed into a stretch, a back leg march or even as a pretend cocked leg! It is great for increasing your dog's awareness of his hindquarters since he has to move his back legs independently. It is also a useful everyday skill, as you can command him to lift his feet when you want to clean or check them after walks.

1 With your dog standing, kneel or crouch down beside him and hold a treat close to his nose. Now move your clicker hand along your dog's body to his hind paw and touch it gently to encourage him to lift it.

2 As soon as your dog lifts his paw, click and give him a treat. Repeat this several times so that your dog understands what you want him to do. Then add in the verbal command, such as 'foot', just before you click.

Key points

● If your dog isn't keen to raise his paw, try tickling between his toes. Many dogs are super-sensitive in this area and will quickly snatch their foot up.

● If your dog still isn't persuaded to lift his paw, pick it up with your hand and then click and treat. Repeat this a few times and he should then understand what you are asking for.

● You can teach hindleg marching using similar steps to the front leg marching training (see page 55). Alternate your left- and right-leg verbal commands – when he has lifted one leg and then the other, click and treat. Gradually add more steps before clicking and rewarding. Raise your leg backwards as you give the verbal cue and you'll soon be marching in unison.

3 Practise the trick, giving your dog the verbal cue and slowly withdrawing the touch on his foot. As he gets the idea, you can try standing up and just giving the verbal command. Then, if you wish, follow the steps through again and teach your dog to raise his other hind paw on a different verbal command.

Say please

Dogs and begging go hand in hand, but, in reality, few pets can actually perform this trick. Your dog needs to learn to balance in a more upright position and this skill will form the foundation of other tricks such as high fives (see page 64) and walking on his hindlegs (see page 68). This trick should be taught only to dogs over six months old in order to avoid placing undue strain on developing hip joints. Even with adult dogs, don't be tempted to relentlessly repeat the more upright tricks and avoid asking for too much too soon.

1 Begin with your dog sitting in front of you, leaving enough space between you for him to raise his front paws off the ground.

2 Holding a treat to your dog's nose, move your hand upwards and push it away from you so that your dog tilts his head backwards. This will encourage him to take his front paws off the ground. As soon as both paws leave the floor, click.

3 Your dog is likely to return his feet to the floor until he gets more balanced – let him do what is comfortable and reward him.

4 Repeat the exercise, each time asking your dog to lift his paws a little bit higher to enable him to find his point of balance. Initially click when your dog has held a position just for a second or two before rewarding. Once your dog can lift his paws and sit back on his haunches fluently, add in a verbal command such as 'both' or 'beg'.

Giving support

Younger dogs and big breeds tend to find it hard to balance in the beg position, so help them initially by supporting a paw – lift their foot and then take the treat over their head to encourage the other paw to follow. Alternatively, they may choose to hold onto your wrist with both paws. This is fine to begin with, but will eventually need to be phased out. Do this by holding the treat in an overhand position (see page 15) with your arm arched up out of reach.

Key points

● If your dog keeps pushing up with his hindlegs into an upright stand, you are asking him to raise his paws too high. Ask for a bit less and click earlier.

● Experiment using an underhand and overhand position (see page 15) to see what works best for you. Underhand positions are often better for younger dogs.

● If your dog tips his head back but doesn't leave the floor, try your 'give paw' command (see page 54) to help him get the idea.

● With tricks like the beg, where you work particularly close to your dog's head, consider using a quieter clicker so you don't hurt his sensitive ears. Alternatively, hold the clicker further away from him or muffle it in a pocket.

● Small dogs usually find it very easy to push up out of a sit and onto their back legs, so they can be tricky to keep on their haunches. Take care not to move the treat very far from their nose, and if necessary, lay your hand on their hindquarters to help discourage them from springing up.

High five!

Celebrate your canine successes in style by teaching your dog a cool high five. This paw-to-hand connection clearly demonstrates a strong dog-and-owner partnership and is bound to bring you a welcome feel-good factor. If your dog can already give a paw (see page 54) and beg (see page 60), this is a straightforward yet impressive trick to teach.

1 With your dog sitting, get down to his level and give your command for 'give paw' (see page 54) while offering your open hand. Click as he touches your hand and reward. Repeat this a few times to build your dog's confidence and momentum in the way he is working.

2 Change to a raised high-five hand and again tell him to 'give paw'. As soon as he touches your raised hand, click and treat. Repeat several times before offering your raised hand, saying 'high five' as your dog makes contact. Click and reward. Practise this until he will happily do the move cued from the 'high five' verbal command.

Key points

● Don't stand so far away when you ask for a full high five that your dog has to tip forwards and overbalances.

● When first teaching the raised hand position, keep your dog thinking and working at a good pace. He is then much more likely to adapt to the new hand position instinctively, without hesitation.

3 Repeat this with the other paw until he is just as fluently tapping your raised hand on this side when you give the 'high five' verbal command.

5 With both hands in the raised position command 'high five'. If he reaches for both hands at the same time, click and reward. If he misses one hand, change your position to improve his chances of making contact with both hands and try again. Practise until perfect.

4 Now stand up and get your dog into the beg position (see page 60).

Stand tall

For some dogs, especially small ones, standing on their hindlegs appears
to be second nature, while bigger breeds can find this move a challenge.
Think about whether your dog's type and build is suited to this trick and
also consider his age and health. Dogs under 12 months old should not
be asked to stand upright. Before you start this trick, make sure your dog
can readily give a paw (see page 54) and practise it a few times.

1 Hold a treat in the overhand position
(see page 15) and get your dog
standing in front of you. Stand or
kneel, depending on the size
of your dog.

2 Ask him to 'give paw' and, as he lifts
his paw, move the treat up and slightly
behind him so that he pushes up onto
his hindlegs. When both front paws
leave the ground with his hindlegs still
in a standing position, click and treat.
Repeat until he understands the task.

Key points

● While 'both' is also used for a beg (see page 60), to your dog it just means raise both front paws – he will simply do this from a sit (for a beg) or stand (to stand tall), as asked.

● Many dogs will find standing still when in an upright position harder than moving slightly, especially to begin with.

3 Gradually increase the height that your dog lifts his paws to improve his balance. Add a command for standing upright, such as 'both'. With practice, aim to achieve a good balanced standing position for a second or two before clicking and treating.

4 If you have a small dog, wait until he is confident with the move before commanding him from a standing position yourself. Little dogs can often feel overpowered if you lean over them and will become reluctant to respond to the command.

Walk tall

If your dog has learned to stand on his hindlegs (see page 66), he should be able to take some steps, too. Many dogs find walking backwards easier by stepping with one foot, then bringing the other paw to meet the first. Try teaching your dog to go backwards first, and if he takes it in his stride, have a go at forwards and sideways moves in addition. You can then try altering your position so that you and your dog walk side by side, for example, instead of facing each other.

1 Get a particularly high-value treat or favourite toy and then ask your dog to stand on his hindlegs.

Key points

● Ensure you click when your dog is actually stepping – he will associate the reward with the movement and it will be easier for him to learn that the action is continuous.

● For moves on the hindlegs, keep practice sessions short. These tricks require concentration, strength and balance, and your dog is likely to tire easily. A tired dog is unlikely to enjoy himself.

● To teach your dog to walk forwards, follow the same process, but stay beside rather than in front of him. Encourage small steps by holding a toy or treat above him and slightly ahead. By facing him and walking backwards with a lure he is more likely to lunge forwards and overbalance.

2 Hold the treat high and walk towards your dog – he will have to take a step backwards. Once he moves a back paw, click and reward. Repeat from the upright stand.

3 As he learns to balance, ask for a second step before clicking and rewarding. Gradually he will learn to walk backwards as you walk towards him. Add in the command 'back' just before clicking so that your dog links this to the movement. As he increases in strength, agility and confidence, he will begin to take larger steps backwards and increase in speed.

High five on high

If you've already taught your dog the basic high five (see page 64) and he is able to balance well on his hindlegs (see page 66), this trick should soon fall into place. Ideally, your dog should be working well on the verbal commands, without a lure.

1 Face your dog and give your command for standing on his hindlegs (see page 66).

Key points

● Don't hold a clicker in your hand for this trick, as a folded hand will confuse your dog. Enlist the help of a friend, use a button clicker (see page 11) or use a verbal signal such as 'yes' instead of a click.

● If your dog puts both his paws onto one of your hands, wait until he separates them before clicking.

● If your dog is struggling to do the high five, practise it in the sitting position (see page 64).

2 Now give your 'high five' command (see page 64) as you show the palms of both your hands. Your dog should reach up and touch his paws to your hands. As soon as he makes contact with one, as long as the other paw is close to your other hand, click and reward. Now practise until he can hit a hand with each paw every time.

Doing the twist

This trick looks great when performed fluently, so increase the level of difficulty gradually – rushing will produce a stilted move or hesitant dog.

1 Stand or kneel in front of your dog and ask him to stand on his hindlegs. Hold a treat in the overhand position (see page 15) above him. Move the treat slowly in a circular motion using just your wrist so that he has to turn his head to watch it.

2 Keep moving the treat in a circular motion so that the dog's body will have to follow his head movement, and he will take a step. Click as soon as he moves a hind foot and reward.

Key points

● Use your right hand for a clockwise twist and the left for an anticlockwise twist, so your dog will know the right direction by the arm you use and can move forwards freely into the twist. If you get confused think about swimming the breaststroke!

● Give your dog plenty of room to learn to twist, so he is not afraid of knocking against anything.

● Teach your dog to twist the way he finds easiest first.

3 Continue in the same way to complete the circle in small steps. As he gets the idea, build up the number of steps he has to do before he is clicked and rewarded and add in the verbal command 'twist'. Once he has achieved a 360-degree twist on a single click, withhold the click until one-and-a-half turns, then two turns and so on to create a continuous pirouette.

Get the low down

This trick can be developed in many fun ways, for example your dog creeping up behind you. But to get your dog to do it well will be a test of your skills. The correct positioning of the lure is crucial and requires you to be able to understand the effect of even tiny movements of your hand on your dog's body posture. Crawling requires your dog to be very agile and supple, so make sure your dog is physically up to the trick. Teach this before the roll over (see page 78) or your dog may spend more time with his legs in the air than creeping along the ground.

1 Introduce your dog to crawling by sitting on the floor with your knees raised and your dog in an upright down (see page 40) at right angles to you. Hold a treat in the hand on the opposite side to your dog and lure him through the tunnel created by your legs while repeating the command 'down'. Click as he is moving under your legs and reward him as he emerges. Practise this several times.

A lesson in luring

The position and movement of the lure is vital for this trick, as this determines how your dog moves his body. A treat held too low will cause your dog to tuck his paws in, twist his head and raise his hindquarters. Moving his reward too fast will cause him to leap up, while too slow will cause frustration because he isn't getting it and doesn't understand what you want as he is receiving no direction.

2 With your dog in an upright down, face him and hold a treat to his nose. Aim to keep his nose approximately 5–7.5 cm (2–3 in) off the floor and his head straight.

3 Move the food steadily away from him, while repeating the 'down' command, but no more than 15 cm (6 in). As soon as your dog edges forwards, while remaining low, click and treat. Practise this, and as he gets the idea, add the command 'crawl' or 'creep' with your repeated 'down' commands, for example, 'down, down, down, crawl', click and treat.

4 Build up the distance your dog crawls by clicking and treating after two shuffles forward, then three and so on. Once he understands the move and can crawl some distance, cut out the 'down' commands. When he can be cued just from the word 'crawl', try standing or moving yourself to develop the trick.

Key points

● Big dogs may be unable to crawl fully, but will creep along with their front end on the ground while they walk with their hindquarters raised.

● If your dog suffers from any joint problems, he is unlikely to be able to do this trick – instead, look for other tricks more suited to his abilities.

● If your dog seems reluctant to crawl, check the type of surface that you are asking him to move along – cold, rough or slippery surfaces will be off-putting.

On a roll

This move will form the basis of 'play dead' (see page 82), so it's worth taking the time to get it really fluent. The floor surface you are asking your dog to roll over on should be comfortable for him so he isn't put off doing the trick. Most dogs learn this move quite easily and may get over-enthusiastic about it, offering roll overs at any opportunity. Once he has got the idea, limit the rehearsals and intersperse this trick with others.

1 Kneel down and position your dog in an upright down (see page 40) in front of you. Hold a treat close to your dog's nose in the underhand position (see page 15).

2 Turn your dog's nose towards his shoulder by moving into the overhand position and arching your arm over his head. If you are rolling your dog onto his left side, use your right hand. Keep moving your dog's nose around and upwards towards the point of his shoulders. Gradually he will become unbalanced.

3 Eventually your dog will reach a point where it is easier for him to flop onto his side, into a flat down (see page 43). Click as he rolls flat and reward him when his head is on the floor.

4 Now repeat the luring pattern above, again moving your hand in a clockwise circle to turn your dog's head towards his side and then up to his shoulder. This time the movement of his head will cause his hindlegs to follow, so he will roll over onto his other side. As soon as his body begins to flip over onto the other side, click. Once he is lying flat, treat.

5 Encourage your dog into an upright down by holding a treat at nose level and moving towards his feet. As he comes up, bring the food towards you. Practise several times before trying to do the roll over in one flowing move, without stopping in the flat positions. In time, add the 'roll over' command before clicking and treating.

Building confidence

Your dog needs to be happy to go into a down before trying any of these more advanced 'floor' moves. A dog that is reluctant to lie down on command is likely to lack confidence and feel vulnerable, and needs to build more trust with his handler. Practise in a relaxed, quiet and comfortable environment with the aim of making the moves fun and easy. Remember that there are no 'wrongs' with clicker training – every lesson should be positive. When working on the roll over, practise Steps 1–3 thoroughly with a more nervous dog before attempting to achieve the full move back to the starting position.

Key points

● Make sure you have the correct hand luring your dog or you could end up in a knot with a rather confused dog!

● Aim to click as your dog rolls but when he is past the point of return. That way you reward the actual movement and it's inevitable that he is going to achieve the full move.

● If your dog finds rolling from the flat down on one side to his other side difficult, help him initially by lifting his front paw nearest the floor.

Dead cool

To achieve the full effect of this trick, your dog needs to drop instantly to the floor and to stay there without a flicker. You can then make this move as detailed as you wish. Before beginning, be sure that your dog can down (see page 40), wait (see page 44) and roll over (see page 78) well. Elements of all these moves are needed for 'dead cool'.

1 Ask your dog to 'roll over', and once he is halfway, command him to 'wait'. As soon as he stops where he is, click and treat. Practise this and gradually extend the amount of time you ask him to wait before clicking and rewarding.

2 To teach your dog to hold his paws upwards or outwards, ask him to give his paw (see page 54) and offer your hand for him to touch. Click as his leg reaches the right point and reward. Work up gradually so that he learns to hold this leg position.

3 Alternatively, practise the flat down position (see page 78). Click either just before your dog rolls or once he has rolled over into the flat position. Treat when his head is on the floor. Add the 'dead' command just before clicking, once he knows the position you want.

Key points

● Work up gradually with the commands you use for this trick to maximize the speed at which your dog drops to the floor. Begin by asking for a 'down, roll over', then 'roll over, wait' before moving on to 'dead, wait'.

● To get your dog to close his eyes, try stroking between his eyes. Click as soon as he shuts them and try to build up the time he keeps them shut by withholding the click. If teaching the flat down version, put him into position and keep him there. When he starts to doze and shuts his eyes, click and treat.

4 Start to cue the trick from a standing position using the 'dead' command. Once he is happily working from this, introduce the hand signal of a gun...

5 ...for the full dramatic effect. With practice, you will be able to drop the verbal command and cue your dog just from the gun hand signal.

Take a bow

All good performers know how to encourage and
acknowledge audience appreciation at the end of a
successful show. Make sure you and your dog finish
your tricks in style with a bow. You can develop this
to become a bow to one another, or a simultaneous
bow to your audience. To create a good bow, you're
aiming for your dog to move as if he is going into a down,
but then holding the position just before his hindquarters sink
to the floor.

1 With your dog standing in front of you, hold
a treat to his nose in the underhand position
(see page 15).

2 Move the food steadily towards your dog and downwards at a 45-degree angle, as if pushing it between his front legs. Aim to tip his nose downwards and backwards, encouraging him to dip his forequarters. As soon as he does hinge backwards and drop, even slightly, click and treat before he drops into a down.

Alternative approaches

If your dog goes into the down position well and you feel confident with the use of the clicker, this trick may be taught in a different way. Simply reward the part of the down manoeuvre that forms the bow by commanding your dog to go down and clicking for the lowered front legs before he drops his hindquarters. Alternatively, the move can be 'captured' from the natural move of stretching – wait until your dog gets up and stretches and click while he is doing the desired movement.

3 Build up the move by withholding the click a little more each time so that your dog keeps dropping a little lower. In time he will drop down onto his elbows while keeping his hindlegs raised. Once your dog can do this, add in the command such as 'bow', 'bend' or 'stretch' before you click and treat. Practise so that the command is linked to the move.

4 Now try the trick with you kneeling and then standing. If your dog can produce the move from just the verbal command, you can then try turning face to face and bowing to each other or even bowing side by side to your audience.

Key points

● Timing is critical – you must click for the drop of the forequarters before your dog is fully committed to going into a down. If you click once he is past the point of return, he will mistakenly think you are rewarding a down.

● For this move your dog needs to be supple through his back, so work up gradually to ensure that he is physically capable.

● Although 'bow' may seem the obvious command to use for this move, consider whether your dog may become confused, as the word 'bow' sounds very similar to the 'down' command.

● If your dog insists on going all the way into a down, break the trick into small steps. Work on just tiny moves of the head and neck first, clicking for a dip of the nose, then lowering the head and so on.

Hide your eyes

This trick is based upon the natural behaviour of a dog when he cleans his face, so you need to find a trigger for him to perform this move. Some dogs are quite sensitive around their face and whiskers, so a light touch may be enough. Others may need a little encouragement, such as a small sticky note stuck onto their fur. Only use items that will come off easily and will not hurt or scare your dog or restrict his breathing.

1 With your dog sitting in front of you, gently place the item you are going to use on his nose. Here the handle loop of a lead is carefully being slid over the dog's muzzle.

2 Command your dog to 'wait' (see page 44) and slowly take your hands away from his face. Get your treat and clicker ready, then give him your release command, allowing him to try to remove the item from his nose.

Key points

● If your dog finds this move tricky, try teaching it from the down position (see page 40). Your dog's paws are then closer to his nose and for some dogs this can be easier.

● Once your dog confidently covers his face on command, you can combine this with other moves, for example, the beg (see page 60) or the bow (see page 84), to produce some fun and effective sequences.

The two-paw hide

To teach your dog to raise both paws to his nose at the same time, place him in a down. Then gently wipe a little bit of soft food onto each side of his muzzle. Allow him to try and rub this off, clicking as soon as he raises either paw to his face and rewarding. Once he has the idea, add in a different verbal command to that used for a single paw, such as 'hide'.

3 When he lifts his paw to brush the item away, click and reward him. Continue to click for each wipe of the paw until the item is removed. Repeat until he understands the movement and then add a verbal command such as 'wipe' or 'face' before you click. Practise until he performs the move from the verbal cue alone. Build up the time he holds his paw in position by delaying the click or commanding him to 'wait'.

Solo catch

This traditional trick is surprisingly difficult to teach. Your dog needs to have good eye-to-mouth coordination, which will only come with practice. Ideally, teach your dog the 'wait' command first (see page 44) so that he will stay still as you place the item on his nose and then wait for your signal. Although the trick can be taught with a treat, it can be more effective to use a flat object such as a plastic lid or small mat. This prevents your dog snatching treats when he hasn't completed the move. Using food to teach the trick can also encourage your dog into short cuts, such as letting the treat conveniently slide off his nose!

1 First, teach your dog to catch. Stand a few steps in front of him, get his attention and then throw a toy or treat for him to catch. If he succeeds, click and treat. If he misses, throw again. Throw accurately and keep practising until your dog is catching more than missing. Then introduce the command 'catch'.

Key points

● Flatter items tend to be easier for your dog to balance, flip and catch. Make sure they are not too heavy.

● Choose an object that is big enough for him to see but not so big that he can't see round it, as he will either refuse to keep it on his nose or be forced to dip his head to see you.

● When balancing the item, encourage your dog to keep his nose level – don't stand over him so that he has to look up to see you.

2 With your dog in sit and wait (see page 44), carefully balance the item on his nose – it mustn't interfere with his eyes. Command 'wait'. After a second or two, click and return to him. Remove the item and reward.

3 Balance the item on his nose and encourage him to flip it up. Make a sharp throwing action and command 'catch'. You want him to jerk his nose up enough to dislodge the item. Click and reward.

4 Keep practising until your dog achieves a catch, then click and reward. If your dog doesn't get the idea, throw him a few toys or treats to catch before balancing one on his nose again. With practice, he will make the connection.

Face to face

You can teach your dog moves that, when put together, become more of a dance routine, like the competitive discipline of heelwork to music. This is great fun and good for keeping you both fit. To move well together, your dog needs to learn to look at you for the next signal, but without being as close as in obedience training. The 'in front' command focuses your dog while keeping him moving.

1 Hold some treats in one hand at waist level, with your clicker in the other hand held in a similar position, so that your elbows are at right angles. When your dog realizes that you have treats, he will come towards you. When he reaches a point a couple of steps away from you and is standing fairly straight, click.

Working on the hard side

Watch to see from which direction of approach your dog tends to achieve a straighter body position, as all dogs will have an 'easier' side. Then work on the opposite one to help him improve flexibility and even up in his movement.

2 Instead of giving him the treat, throw it out to your side. Aim for it to land on the floor at least 2 m (6 ft 6 in) away from you. Your dog will go to get the treat.

3 Once he has eaten that treat, he will return to see if you have any more. As he does so he will start to look up to your hands or face.

4 He may stop initially at right angles to you or he may swing round to stand straight in front you. Click when he steps his hindlegs round to bring his body straight so that he is facing you. Then throw his treat to the opposite side to repeat the exercise again. Gradually ask for a straighter body position and a faster return to you by withholding the click.

5 Continue to repeat the exercise so that your dog learns that it is how he returns to you that is important. Then try turning 90 degrees away from your dog each time you have thrown the reward. This will compel him to flex and step around more to position himself in front of you. Once your dog is positioning himself squarely in front of you, add the 'in front' command just before you click and reward.

Key points

● Aim to get your dog returning to you, placing his front paws in front of you and then smartly swinging round on his hindlegs to straighten his body and improve his back-end awareness (see page 39).

● Work in an area where the floor is clear so that your dog can easily find his reward and is unlikely to find anything else tempting. He will then quickly realize that you are the best source of treats.

Move along

Once you have taught the 'in front' position (see page 92), it can be developed into sidestepping. Review the 'in front' position, then start to sidestep while keeping a rhythm. If you can, take a step to the side, then cross your other leg in front before taking another sidestep. Take three steps to the side, then kick to the side before changing direction.

1 First, practise this exercise based on a clock face, to help your dog separate the movement he needs to make with his hindquarters from that of his forequarters. Imagine you are at the centre of a clock face and your dog is one of the hands. Start at two o'clock and, as you give the command 'in front', swivel round to face four o'clock.

2 Aim for your dog to take big sideways steps with his hindlegs. Click for the strongest ones and reward. Now move round to six and eight o'clock in the same way, before trying the movements in an anticlockwise direction. Observe which way your dog finds easiest.

Key points

● Dogs tend to favour one side. On the 'easier' side, they will tend to cross their hindlegs, while on the other (usually right) they may step the foot up to the other one but not cross it. Practise all exercises regularly in both directions.

● Do this move to some upbeat music and with a spring in your step to help you keep a good rhythm and add to the fun.

● Try to click when your dog's hindquarters are in line with the centre of your body, and make your sideways steps decisive and active to encourage him to move positively.

3 Take a sidestep in the direction your dog finds easiest. Command 'in front' with your hands positioned as before for that move (see Step 1, page 92). As he steps across with his hindlegs, click and treat.

4 Repeat the move until he steps across equally with his front and back legs. Ask for two steps before clicking and treating. As he improves, gradually increase the number of steps and the speed, and start changing direction.

Round the twist

It is important to teach this move with the correct hand for each side of the body to ensure that your dog keeps travelling forwards as well as doing a twist. He will move forwards into the turn and come out of it facing the right direction to continue onwards. This will also allow you to indicate which direction twist you want by the hand you use.

1 With your dog standing in front of you, hold a treat to his nose with your right hand. Encourage him to turn his head to the right by moving the treat level with his nose backwards as far as his shoulder. Once he has flexed this far, click and treat.

2 Now lure his head round further towards his tail, until he takes a step with his front feet. As he steps, click and reward.

Key points

● Once your dog can complete a full twist, encourage him to keep twisting by withholding the click to a twist-and-a-quarter, two twists and so on.

● Teach the move in the opposite direction, using the opposite hand to lure and a separate command – 'twist' for a clockwise turn and 'spin' for an anticlockwise turn.

3 This time, ask for more of a turn by luring your dog's nose past his tail position so that he has to step round with front and hindlegs. As soon as he passes the halfway mark, click. From here your dog is likely to continue the circle of his own accord so that he comes round to face you and so receive his reward. Once he is facing you and standing straight, reward.

4 Repeat until your dog can complete a full circle, clicking at the halfway point and rewarding as he faces you. You should soon be able to stop using a lure and just use your hand. Add the command 'twist' or 'spin' before you click and treat. Stand up, command 'twist' and without a hand signal your dog will spin on the spot.

Sticking around

This move forms the basis of other moves, such as circling around one leg (see page 110) or a cane (see page 122), and helps prepare him for more complicated tricks, such as weaving through your legs (see page 114). To teach your dog to circle around you fluently, you must make sure you are able to transfer the lure you use quickly and smoothly between hands. If you hesitate or fumble, your dog will lose the flow of movement or become distracted or confused.

1 Before you start working with your dog, practise passing your lure, hand to hand, in front and behind your body, clockwise and anticlockwise. Then begin with your dog standing at heel on your left side (see page 48). Hold the treat and clicker in your right hand and lure your dog across the front of you, around your right side.

2 Bring your dog around behind you and smoothly switch your lure from one hand to the other, keeping your dog moving.

Keeping it positive

Tune the length of your practice sessions to your dog. If he is happy and enjoying himself, continue, but make sure you call an end to the session while things are still going well – your dog will then be keen to come back for more. If things are going badly, he could be confused, bored or tired. Change to a trick your dog knows well, perform it once and reward him. You can then finish the session on a high note and come back to the harder task when you are both feeling fresh.

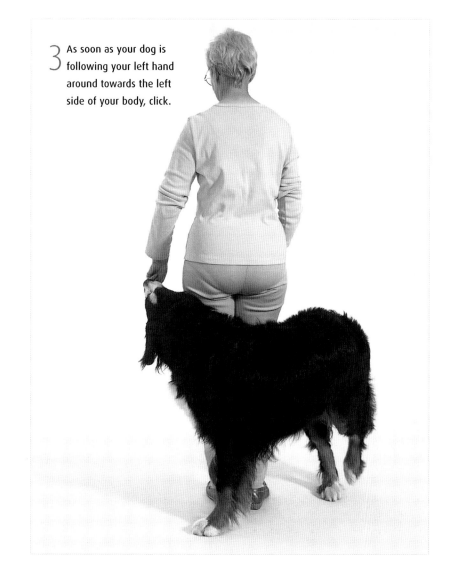

3 As soon as your dog is following your left hand around towards the left side of your body, click.

Key points

● If passing the treats from one hand to the other proves tricky, try having some in each hand.

● For this type of move, using a toy can be more effective and easier than food, as long as your dog responds well to it.

● Teach this move in the opposite direction, too, using the opposite hand sequence. Use a different voice command so that you can signal which way you wish your dog to move.

● With a small dog, it may be easier to teach this move from a kneeling position.

● Once your dog is circling well around you, you can vary the trick by simultaneously turning in the opposite direction to him.

4 Bring him back to his starting position beside you to complete the circle, and treat. Repeat this sequence two or three times, each time clicking after you transfer the lure to the other hand, but treating at different points in the circle, not just at heel. Now add in the verbal command 'round' and gradually stop luring with food or a toy, just making the same hand movements to direct your dog. Once your dog has learned the voice command, you can then fade out the hand signals if you wish.

The magic circle

This trick looks as if your dog is connected to you by invisible string. How wide a circle he traces will depend on the space available and the size of circle you teach him initially. Having taught him to circle close to you (see page 100), you now need to teach him to move further away. This is best done with a puppy pen (see page 12), which gives a solid but see-through barrier that can be adjusted to various shapes and sizes.

1 Set up your pen in a wide circle and get into it. Lure your dog around the outside of the pen by walking around the perimeter with a treat. (For larger circles, use two pens joined together.)

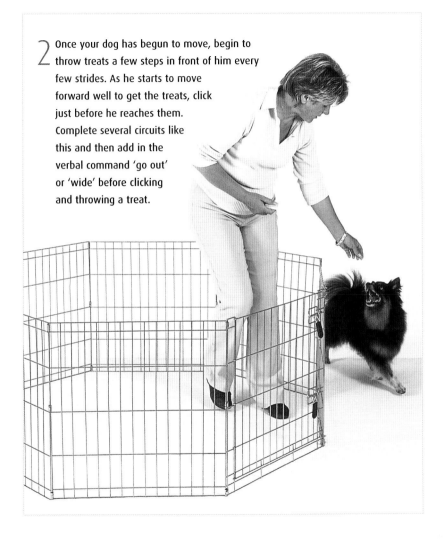

2 Once your dog has begun to move, begin to throw treats a few steps in front of him every few strides. As he starts to move forward well to get the treats, click just before he reaches them. Complete several circuits like this and then add in the verbal command 'go out' or 'wide' before clicking and throwing a treat.

3 When he understands the command, try rotating in the centre of the pen. Give the voice command, click as your dog moves, throwing treats ahead of him to maintain the movement. Once the movement is flowing, vary the amount of food you throw. For example, after half a circle, click and treat, then a circle-and-a-half, then one circle, then two. This will teach your dog to continue circling until you tell him otherwise.

Key points

● Don't worry if you throw the food wide as long as it is in front of your dog, as he will soon return to circling again.

● If your dog insists on coming close to you once you remove the pen, put the barrier back in place and practise a little more.

● Teach this trick moving in both directions, giving a different command for each.

Adding a counter-turn

Develop this trick by turning in a circle yourself, in the opposite direction to your dog. When first introducing this movement, wait until he has just gone past your line of sight to the side and turn half a circle. Repeat this until you can start to turn full circles without distracting your dog.

4 When he can circle from a verbal cue, try the move without the pen. Keep him out wide by always clicking at the furthest point he reaches and throwing a treat to him. If he keeps coming in close, throw a treat out to move him away, then click just before he reaches it.

Through the legs

As well as needing to be flexible and able to move well to perform some of the more complex tricks, a dog needs to be confident that his owner is careful and isn't about to stand on him. This trick helps both to establish trust and improve suppleness.

1 With your dog in a wait in front of you (see page 44), stand with your legs wide enough apart for your dog to fit through comfortably. Place a treat through your legs and onto the floor 2.5–5 cm (1–2 in) behind you. Call your dog, and as soon as his nose goes through your legs but before he gets the treat, click. If he reverses back after getting his reward, don't worry.

2 Repeat, gradually placing or throwing the food further behind you until your dog goes right through your legs. Click as he passes under you. As he gets his food, turn to face him and throw another treat through your legs so that your dog passes back under you the other way. Repeat this to encourage your dog to move quickly. Once he is confident, add the command 'through' before you click.

through the legs **109**

Round one leg

This helps to build the confidence that is essential if your dog is to learn to move around your legs as you are moving – for example, weaving through your legs as you walk (see page 114) – as well as improving his flexibility.

1 To circle the left leg, begin with your dog on your left side. Holding the clicker in your right hand and treats in both hands, lure your dog around the front of you and then between your legs. Switch your dog from the food in your right to that in your left hand, and as soon as he goes through your legs, click.

Key points

● Make it easy for your dog by giving him plenty of room and making the route clear by keeping your hair, head, clothing and arms out of the way.

● Aim for your dog to come through your legs straight, quickly and cleanly.

● Try using a button clicker (see page 11), which can be operated more easily within your hand or with your foot when you are holding treats.

2 Bring him around your left side with your left hand until he is back where he started and treat. Repeat several times. Once he gets the idea, reduce the luring and click and treat at different points of the circle for continuous movement. Add the

command 'through, round' so that he knows to go through your legs first, then circle. When he links the move to the command, he should be able to do it with you standing upright. You can then teach him to circle your right leg anticlockwise, using the reverse hand sequence.

Ins and outs

First, ensure your dog is confident circling around each of your legs (anticlockwise around the right leg and clockwise around the left – see page 110) and going through them (see page 108). This helps to avoid problems such as your dog missing out part of the figure-of-eight move or being unsure of the pattern you want. This first weave is the basis for various weave tricks, including those performed on the move.

1 With your dog on your left, lure him around the front of your left leg using a treat in your left hand. Switch him over to follow the treat in your right hand, behind your right knee, to encourage him through your legs.

2 Lure him with your right hand around your right leg. Then lure with your left hand, behind your left knee, to lead him back through your legs. Click as he passes under and bring him around your left leg with your left hand to the starting point and treat. Practise so the move flows. Vary where and how soon you click and treat, and add in the command 'weave'.

Key points

● To help your dog weave through your legs, flex the knee that you want him to go behind forwards. This makes the gap a little bit clearer and more inviting to him.

● Initially, aim to click as your dog passes under your legs for the second time, to complete the figure-of-eight.

● As you first teach the weave, make sure you don't move the hand holding the treat too fast, as your dog will try to cut corners to get it.

3 As your dog gets the idea, you can use less food and just give the hand signals. When he is working well from the verbal command, you can stand up and cut down the hand signals.

4 Keep practising and your dog will get faster and be able to weave around your legs from just the verbal command.

Weave walking

For this trick to look good, concentrate on your own body position. Don't slump or shuffle; instead walk tall, proud and with purpose. Before beginning, make sure your dog can weave on the spot (see page 112) from your voice command. This avoids you having to lean down and lure your dog while standing on one leg.

1 Begin with your dog on your left. Raise your right leg and command 'weave'. As your dog passes under your leg, begin to make the step forward.

2 As your right foot reaches the floor, command 'weave' again to encourage your dog to come back under your other leg.

3 Raise your left leg and click as your dog passes underneath. Reward once he reaches your left side again. Build up the number of steps before clicking and treating on either side of you.

Sidestep weaving

To begin with, you will need to slow things down to let your dog get
an idea of what's required, so practise walking a step at a time,
balancing on each leg in turn. Your dog won't appreciate you wobbling
about or falling over him.

1 With your dog on your left,
raise your right leg in front
of you, telling your dog to
'weave'. As he passes under
your leg, swing it behind
him and step sideways to
your left.

Key points

● Always hold the leg you wish your dog to pass under out in front of you. It can seem easier to step forwards and leave a leg behind for your dog to weave under, but this looks messy and awkward once you begin to speed up.

● If you get mixed up with your steps, practise these first before trying them with your dog.

2 Lift your left leg in front of you, commanding 'weave', so that he passes under this leg in the opposite direction. As he goes under, click. Then cross your left leg in front of your right to sidestep again to the right. As your dog turns to come to you, treat. Gradually build up this sequence and practise in both directions.

sidestep weaving **117**

Kick it!

To do this fun move, you need to be quick on your feet, but your dog doesn't have to be so fast to weave correctly. Before you start, read the steps, as they are different to sideways weaving (see page 116) and need more coordination. Try to move in a good rhythm by saying to yourself '1-2-3 kick', then put on some music and strut your stuff!

1 With your dog on your right, kick your left leg out in front of you and command him to 'weave'.

2 As your dog goes under your left leg, bring it across your right leg to sidestep to your right.

3 Take another step to your right with your right leg.

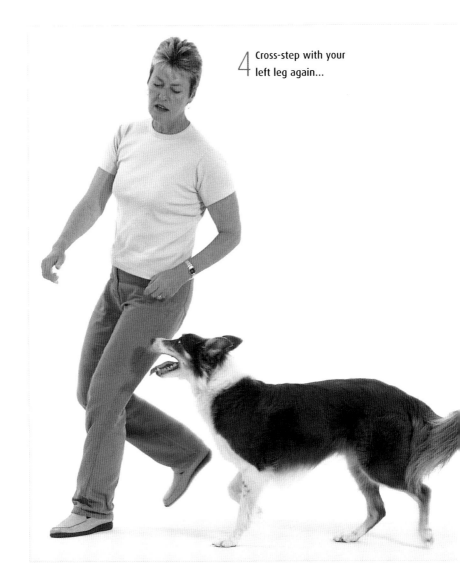

4 Cross-step with your left leg again...

5 ...and finish with a right-leg kick to the front, commanding your dog to 'weave'. Then simply cross-step with your right leg to the left to repeat the sequence in the opposite direction. Phew!

Key points

● Start slowly and build up the speed once your dog understands what you want.

● To begin with, click and treat once your dog has completed the second weave. Then increase the exercise so that you move in both directions before clicking and so on.

● If your dog gets too excited, work through a couple of calmer exercises before doing this one again.

● Be very careful not to tread on your dog's feet.

Pole position

By introducing your dog to working with a pole, you can begin to add in all sorts of extras to your tricks. You can get your dog to jump it, go under it, go round it or even use it to give directions or create new movements. To begin with, the pole will be used to introduce tricks that you can later perform with a cane. At this stage, it is vital to use a free-standing pole to avoid confusing your dog and allow you two free hands. You can either buy poles with cone bases from agility suppliers or make your own version (see page 13).

1 With the pole and your dog on your right, lure your dog away from you and around the far side of the pole with your right hand.

2 Encourage him all the way round and click just before he completes the circle, then reward. Repeat this several times, building up to two or three circles before clicking and rewarding. Add the command 'circle pole' or 'pole' before clicking.

Performance planning

Think about how you plan to use a trick before you teach it. By teaching the circles as described here, you can walk, plant your cane and circle in the opposite direction to your dog. If you teach the opposite ways, you will have to turn around and change hands, and the move will not flow.

3 Now cut down your hand movements until your dog will still circle with your hand just resting on the top of the pole.

4 Once your dog understands the move and the verbal command in one direction, teach the other side. On your left, your dog should circle the pole clockwise.

5 Once your dog is confident with the move, you can try moving in a circle in the opposite direction to him. When this is fluent, you can have a go with a proper cane.

Key points

● Teach this trick with a free-standing pole. It isn't possible to lure your dog and hold the pole upright without getting in a big tangle and confusing your dog.

● Toys can be better lures for this trick, as they are more visible.

● Teach the circle moves around you first (see page 104) so that your dog already understands the basic idea.

Swing it!

Teach this move using two free-standing poles initially, so your dog learns the figure-of-eight pattern. He should already be able to circle one pole and understand that the direction he circles depends on which side of your body you hold the pole (see page 122). By linking these skills together one flowing move will be created.

1 Stand between and slightly behind the two poles, spaced so that you can comfortably reach past both of them. With your dog on your left and the lure in your left hand, lead him clockwise round the left pole, commanding 'pole' or 'circle pole'.

2 As your dog turns back towards you, switch him onto the lure in your right hand. Lead him anticlockwise round the right pole and again command 'pole'.

3 As he comes round to face you, lead your dog across to the other pole by swapping him back onto the lure in your left hand. Take him around the left pole, and as he reaches his starting point, click and reward. Repeat, building up how much he has to do to get a click. With practice, you will be able to reduce the luring and hand movement until you can simply put your hand on the top of the pole that you wish your dog to circle.

4 Once your dog knows to circle the pole that your hand is on, try using a cane. First hold it out to your right and command 'pole' so that your dog circles it...

5 ...then switch the cane to the other hand across your body...

6 ...before placing the pole to your left and commanding your dog so that he circles in the opposite direction.

Key points

● In time, you will be able to drop the verbal command completely, as the positioning of the cane will cue your dog.

● Once your dog has learned the trick, you can try different props, such as an umbrella.

● If your dog is new to circling moves or is unsure of what you are asking for, break the move down into small steps. Send your dog around the left pole and click as he returns to you and reward. Then send him around the right pole, clicking as he comes back towards you and treating. You can then link the two circles together.

Backtrack

Tricks and sequences involving backward moves look dramatic, and many dogs will learn to reverse quite quickly. As well as being good for performing, a dog who can reverse easily will be less cumbersome in the house, as he will be able to manoeuvre out of your path more readily. Reversing can be taught in several different ways.

Method 1

In this approach, food is used to prompt the behaviour, while the dog is allowed to work out what is required by himself.

1 With your feet wide enough apart for your dog to fit between them, place a treat between your heels. Let your dog come and get it. Once he has eaten it, he is likely to step backwards so that he can look up to your hands or face to see if more food is coming.

Key points

● If your dog stops moving backwards before you have clicked, either wait to see if he begins to move back again or restart the behaviour with another treat. Don't ever be tempted to walk backwards yourself, as this will only encourage your dog forwards.

● Don't put food too far through your legs to begin with, as your dog is likely to go right through.

● This method is particularly good for small dogs who will have to reverse quite a few steps to be able to get you in sight.

2 As soon as he takes a step back, click and reward with a treat placed between your feet. Repeat and when he reverses back to look at you, withhold the click. He will likely reverse to the same point, expecting a click, but when none comes, try another step or two back. Click when he does this and reward again between your feet. Continue to increase the number of steps in this way. Once he is walking backwards well, add the command 'walk back', then gradually cut out the treat.

Method 2

In this method, you use your body position and hand movement to 'push' your dog into walking backwards.

1 With your dog standing in front of you, hold a treat to his nose. Keeping your hand level, make a quick, firm but gentle pushing movement with the food into your dog's muzzle. You are aiming to encourage him to tuck his head backwards into his neck.

Keeping on the straight and narrow

To help keep your dog straight as he reverses, use the 'in front' command (see page 92) where your dog learnt to move his hindlegs in line with his front legs. Alternatively, make a channel using a puppy pen (see pages 12 and 134). Get him confident moving forwards through the channel first, then as he reverses he will have a low fence on either side to guide him back.

2 At the same time, step towards your dog – your body and hand movement should encourage him to move backwards. As soon as he takes a step, click and treat. Practise, gradually increasing the number of steps, and then add in the 'walk back' command.

Key points

● Keeping a good hand position is critical – too high and your dog will sit; too low and he will simply lie down.

● Your hand needs to move at the right speed – too slow and your dog will just sit or not move at all.

Reversing in tandem

As well as reversing away from you, you can teach your dog to reverse with you. This trick is best taught using a puppy pen (see page 12), set up to form a channel, so your dog has a clear guideline of how and where you want him to move, and allowing him to work out the rest by himself. He is then likely to be rewarded more easily and so learn the task more efficiently.

1 Use a puppy pen to form a channel wide enough for you and your dog to stand within it, side by side. Place your dog in the heel position on your left (see page 48) and hold a treat to his nose.

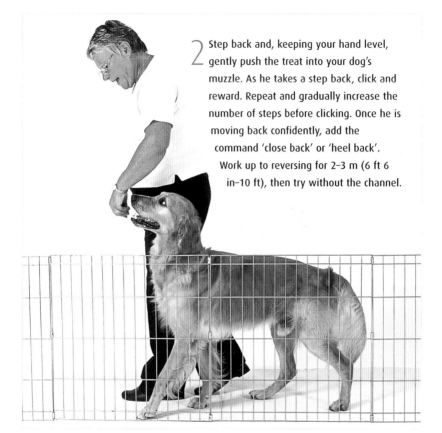

2 Step back and, keeping your hand level, gently push the treat into your dog's muzzle. As he takes a step back, click and reward. Repeat and gradually increase the number of steps before clicking. Once he is moving back confidently, add the command 'close back' or 'heel back'. Work up to reversing for 2–3 m (6 ft 6 in–10 ft), then try without the channel.

Key points

● Step back confidently yourself.

● If your dog starts to tuck behind you or swings out, practise again with the pen.

● Repeat your command regularly to help straighten your dog, once you have moved out of the puppy-pen channel.

Reversing in the round

A puppy pen is used here again to guide movement, but once the basics are in place you can move on to trying the trick in the open.

1 Create a pen that gives your dog enough room to move around when you stand in the middle. Walk him forwards around you to get him used to the restricted space. Then, from the left heel position, command 'back' but stay still. If necessary, encourage your dog to step backwards by gently moving a treat into his nose.

2 As his nose emerges past your right leg, click and give him a treat on your right side. Repeat for the second half of the circle. Build up to your dog completing a full circle before clicking and then withhold the click to achieve several circles in succession. Add a verbal command, such as 'reverse', or 'back up, around'.

Key points

● Adjust the size of the pen to suit the size of your dog.

● Make sure you allow enough room in the pen behind you for your dog to reverse.

● If you do not have a pen, use a corner of your kitchen or any other room. You can then teach half a circle of reversing at a time, with your dog moving between you and the corner.

3 Once your dog can do multiple circles around you in the pen, try without it. If he achieves this, then move on to teaching him the move in the opposite direction, using the same method shown in Steps 1 and 2.

Back up

This trick is really several moves that have all been taught separately and are then linked together to achieve the full effect. To be able to perform the complete sequence, your dog needs to be able to reverse away from you on command, make a half turn and reverse between your legs. Teach each of these things thoroughly and don't try to do the whole lot at once, or your dog will feel bombarded. A more gradual approach will achieve a much better, lasting result.

Sound support

As your dog backs up, he will struggle to see where you are unless he turns his head, although some dogs do try hard to use their peripheral vision.

Therefore, help him locate you with sound by repeating the 'back up' command – some dogs will rely heavily on sound for this move.

1 First teach your dog to reverse through your legs. Stand astride him and, with a treat to his nose, 'push' him gently backwards. Click as he goes through your legs and treat him when he returns to your side. Repeat this until he does it without the 'push', then add the command 'back up'.

2 Gradually increase the distance you ask your dog to reverse to reach you. Begin just a stride away – give the command and click as your dog goes through your legs, rewarding once he is at your side again. Then build up by telling your dog to 'stand, wait' and walking back behind him, adding a stride at a time until he can reverse to you across a room.

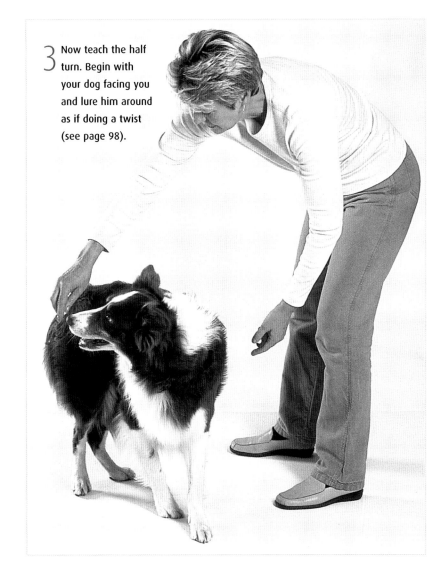

3 Now teach the half turn. Begin with your dog facing you and lure him around as if doing a twist (see page 98).

Key points

● Your dog is likely to reverse into you to begin with, so try to move to accommodate him.

● Keep your turn tidy to increase the chances of your dog reversing accurately to you.

● As you link the components of the trick together, watch for signs that your dog doesn't understand. It is better to slow down a little or return to the previous step and get minor problems ironed out before they become major ones.

4 Once your dog is facing away from you, click and throw a treat in front of him so he doesn't have to do a full circle to get the reward. If he continues past 180 degrees, put your hand on his hindquarters to stop him. Practise and add in the command 'turn'. Once your dog turns on command, link it to the back up. With your dog in a 'stand, wait', move a few steps ahead of him. Tell him to 'turn' and then 'back up', clicking as he passes through your legs. Establish this, then add the commands 'walk back', 'turn' and finally 'back up'.

Jump to it!

Teaching your dog to jump is fun. Start low, so your dog learns how to take off and land correctly, without risking injury. You can then gradually increase the height of the obstacles. Don't push your dog too much – a jump of 0.7 m (2 ft 6 in) is plenty even for a large, fit dog with agility experience. Consider your dog's age, fitness and health, and if in any doubt, ask your vet to check him over before take-off.

Staying focused

For a dog to jump well, his front paws should take off first and land first. To do this, he must be looking in the direction he is travelling. You often see dogs landing either with all four feet together or hindlegs first – this is because they are looking up to their owner, rather than concentrating on the job in hand. As a result, they may hit the obstacle or land poorly, increasing the risk of injury. It will also lose time in agility competitions.

1 Set up a jump 5–15 cm (2–6 in) high so that your dog can easily get over but cannot get under. Tell him to wait (see page 44) while you step over the jump and take a couple of strides before turning to face him. Recall him excitedly with your arms held wide, clicking as he jumps and treating once he reaches you. Repeat several times, adding in the command 'over'.

2 Tell your dog to wait and place a treat on the ground on the opposite side of the jump, where you were standing.

Return to your dog, ready to run beside him. The treat will encourage him to look ahead rather than at you.

3 Release and run with him as he goes over the jump to get the treat. Click as he jumps. Practise this and then send him over the jump without running beside him. Gradually stop using the treats and do several jumps before rewarding your dog.

Key points

● If your dog goes around the jump, start with him a little closer and make the jump smaller or lay the pole on the floor.

● Once your dog learns 'over', take care with your command timing. Some dogs will try to jump straight over an obstacle when commanded, even if they are at a distance from it. Either send your dog into the jump from slightly further away by saying 'go over' or only say 'over' when he is within reach of the fence.

● If your dog ducks under a fence when you raise the height, lower the pole again and practise more to improve his confidence.

Spread your wings

To teach your dog to jump over your arm, you need a helper, to show him what is required and help him to jump accurately. He needs to leap over your arm, not just your hand, and to look forwards rather than at you. Get together with a dog-owning friend so you can both benefit, and even try getting both dogs to jump at once.

1 Ask your helper to kneel and hold their arm out straight and low. With your dog in a wait (see page 44), hold a treat close to his nose. Release him and run, aiming to stay a step ahead, using your body position to guide him over the outstretched arm. Click as he jumps and reward when he catches up. Repeat several times.

2 If your dog is confident, ask your helper to gradually raise their arm height until it is at shoulder level. Practise jumping in both directions and on both sides of your helper's body.

3 Position your dog in a wait in front of your helper, and go behind them so that you are taking your dog across the outstretched arm. Call your dog towards you and command 'over', clicking as he jumps the arm and rewarding as he reaches you. Practise this so that your dog jumps accurately.

Tricks for two

Once your dog is confident jumping, you can teach him all sorts of variations for more effective tricks. If you have two dogs, try asking one dog to 'down, wait' while the other circles you, jumping the first dog. Make sure the dogs are of suitable sizes and temperaments first.

4 Now you or your helper can try the trick alone. With your dog in a wait, kneel several strides in front of him and raise your arm. Command your dog 'over', clicking as he jumps your arm and throwing rewards ahead of him.

Key points

● Keep a stride ahead of your dog when running with him, to give him room to see the jump and judge the distance. If your hand is less than 15 cm (6 in) from his nose, he will only focus on the treat.

● If your dog dives around your helper's outstretched arm, reposition yourself so that your dog is channelled over the jump.

● You can build up the trick so that your dog jumps one arm in one direction and your other arm back again. Use a helper to show him how to make the turn.

Ring master

Teach your dog to jump through a hoop as a trick in itself or as the starting point to jumping through your arms. Once he knows what the hoop is for, you can build up sequences where he moves around you, jumping through the hoop each time you present it.

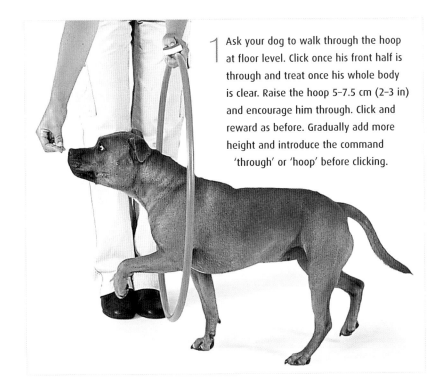

1 Ask your dog to walk through the hoop at floor level. Click once his front half is through and treat once his whole body is clear. Raise the hoop 5–7.5 cm (2–3 in) and encourage him through. Click and reward as before. Gradually add more height and introduce the command 'through' or 'hoop' before clicking.

2 Encourage your dog to jump higher and faster by asking him to wait and throwing a treat on the floor on the opposite side of the hoop. Release him and command 'hoop', clicking as he jumps through. With practice, you will be able to drop the verbal command, as simply holding out the hoop will cue your dog.

Jumping duo

When your dog is confident with jumping through a hoop, try this harder jump through your arms. You'll need someone to help you teach this trick, but the end result is a great illustration of you and your dog's teamwork and trust in one another.

1 Ask your dog to 'sit, wait' and position yourself a few paces in front of him. Make a big hoop with your arms, low to the ground, and ask your helper to stand on the landing side and show your dog a treat through the centre of the circle, with the hand nearest to your dog. Command 'hoop', and as soon as your dog takes off to go through your arms, click. Your helper then throws the food to land a few paces ahead of your dog. Repeat.

Key points

● Avoid wearing baggy clothes or having floppy hair when asking your dog to jump through your arms – he needs to be able to see a clear space to jump through.

● Whether holding out a hoop or your arms, keep a steady position so that your dog can judge where he is expected to jump.

● The higher you are asking your dog to jump, the bigger run-up you need to give him.

2 Using the same method, slowly add more height. When you click, your helper should keep throwing treats in front of your dog to keep him focused and moving forwards.

3 If he is confident going through your arms towards your helper and knows the verbal command, try the trick without encouragement from your friend. Put a treat on the floor on the landing side. Make a hoop with your arms and ask him to jump. As he jumps, click. Practise until your arm position becomes the cue to jump.

Get a wiggle on

If you want your dog to be a flexible friend, there is no better exercise than this. The weave poles are a highlight of every agility ring, with the best dogs appearing to be just a blur as they complete this task. To get to this level takes lots of practice, but even doing this exercise steadily will improve your dog's coordination and ability to bend.

1 Begin with your dog at your right side at one end of the poles. You will walk along the left side of the poles while your dog goes in and out of them. Lure him away from you and anticlockwise around the first pole, bringing him between the first and second pole. Then go clockwise around the second pole, between the second and third pole, and so on along the line.

Fast-tracking

To focus your dog on travelling straight through the poles, the exercise is often taught with the poles set up in two lines just wide enough for the dog to fit through the middle, within the channel. Once the dog has learned to travel down the centre of them, they are moved closer so that he has to wiggle his body slightly. This is increased until he has to slalom fully, but he is focused on getting through the poles rather than on moving from side to side.

2 As his nose goes between the last pair of poles, click, rewarding as he clears them completely. Repeat this several times.

3 As your dog gets the idea, he should be happy to just follow your hand for guidance. Add the command 'weave' for each turn about a pole.

4 Click as he goes between the last two poles, and throw the treat ahead of your dog to encourage him to come through the poles faster. Practise this, building up speed and reducing your hand signals, until you can just move your hand in a straight line and give the command. Eventually even the visual cue can be dropped.

Key points

● While luring, keep your dog's head level so that he can still see the poles.

● As you build up speed, your dog will change from trotting to doing a two-footed jump between each of the poles.

● Always send your dog into the weave poles the same way.

Follow your leader

Clicker training encourages a dog to use his foot, nose or mouth on cue
to work out the tasks you set. This is done by using 'targets' that the
dog is trained to touch with a specific part of his body. The target can
be moved and used in various situations to transfer the behaviour to
other items or to teach complex moves. Start by teaching your dog to
place his nose on or close to your hand. This will help you to guide
him through moves such as heelwork without the use of luring.

1 Place a piece of food
between your second and
third fingers. It needs to
be visible from the back of
your hand, but firmly held
so that your dog can sniff
it yet not get it.

2 Hold the back of your hand out so that your
dog sniffs at the treat. When his nose touches
your hand, click and move your target hand up
and out of his reach. Give a treat from your
other hand before presenting your target hand
again slightly in front of him so that he comes
to sniff it again. Click and treat as before.

Three types of target

1 Your hand A good starting point, suitable for close work such as heeling and twists. It takes away the need to hold a toy or treat.

2 Target stick An extendable stick (see pages 12 and 158) used to teach wider circle moves and standing on hindlegs. Can be used to raise your dog's movement for a high-stepping trot.

3 Target marker Usually a flat object such as a mat, plastic lid or piece of wood (see pages 12 and 160). The marker can be moved onto another object to show your dog how and where you want him to touch it.

Key points

● If your dog doesn't touch the target within three seconds of you presenting it, move it out of reach again. Then re-present your target hand, showing the food in it, and encouraging your dog by asking 'what's this?'.

● Once your dog follows a target, make sure you continue to click and treat at intervals to maintain his motivation.

3 Gradually ask your dog to move further to touch your hand and throw his treats a little way from you. Give your hand without a treat – if he still touches it, click and treat. Repeat and add a verbal command like 'pat' or 'nose.' Build up how far he moves before clicking, until you can move your hand in any direction and he follows.

Targeted moves

Teaching your dog to move to a target is all about telling him exactly what, where and how you want him to interact with an object. The target stick and marker are both used for this, but each works better for different situations. The target stick is good for creating movement in a specific direction.

Nose target

Stick a small ball on the end of the target stick to make it more visible and easier to touch. With the clicker and target stick in the same hand, hold the stick out near your dog. As soon as his nose touches it to sniff, click. Throw a treat in the opposite direction so that he then has to move back to the stick to touch it again. Practise, then add the command 'pat' before clicking.

Stand and bow

Once your dog has learned to follow the target stick fluently, it opens up many other ways of encouraging moves. Simply lift the stick up for a stand on back legs or move it down between the dog's legs for a bow. It will also allow you to achieve more accurate circle moves or teach a high-stepping trot.

Paw moves

Use a different end on your target stick to cue paw moves – ideally a flat, rectangular-shaped piece of plastic or wood that will support his paw. Hold it out to him and give your 'give paw' command (see page 54). Click as he touches, treat and repeat. Remember to always keep nose and paw targets separate.

Hitting the mark

The target marker is used to tell your dog to 'go to' a specific place or touch an item at a particular point or in a particular way. As with the target stick, the target marker can be taught as paw- or nose-specific.

1 Choose a small mat or plastic lid to be a nose marker. Place it on the floor, and with your dog in a wait (see page 44), place a treat on top of the marker.

2 Encourage him to get the treat and click when his nose touches the marker. Practise and add the command 'nose'. Then try with no treat on the mat. If he touches it, click and throw a treat away from the mat, then repeat. If he doesn't, place a treat on the mat a few more times.

3 Use a larger mat with a treat on the side furthest away from your dog. From a wait position, encourage him to get the treat. As he steps onto the mat with both front feet to reach the food, click. Practise and add the command 'on your mark'. Then try without a treat on the mat. If he stands on the mat with two feet, click and reward. If not, practise a bit more.

Fetch and carry

Playing and interacting with your dog is a vital part of dog ownership, but it is much harder if he clears off with his toys and refuses to bring them back. Teaching him to retrieve will solve this and add to your trick repertoire. Gun dogs have this behaviour 'in their blood', while toy breeds are frequently 'mealy-mouthed'. Take this into account as well as your dog's preferences for what he holds in his mouth. While some will carry anything, others will only pick up soft or rubber toys. It is easiest to teach retrieving if your dog already understands nose targeting (see page 158).

1 Show your dog the retrieve item, click as he sniffs it and treat. Repeat. Now hold out the toy again, but don't click this time until he mouths it, then treat.

2 Gradually wait a little longer each time before clicking to encourage your dog to keep hold of the toy. Once he holds it for a couple of seconds, try letting go of it yourself. Click before your dog drops the toy and treat. If he drops the toy, wait to see if he picks it up. If he does, click and treat.

3 Put the toy on the floor. If your dog picks it up, click and treat. If not, practise Step 2 a little more. Once your dog is confidently picking up the toy and holding it, try placing it a little further away.

4 Wait until your dog makes a step towards you holding the toy before clicking. Your dog is likely to drop the toy to come and get his treat. Now wait to see if your dog goes back to the toy. If he picks it up, let him take another step towards you before clicking and repeating the process again.

Leave lessons

While it is common for a dog to be taught to leave and retrieve at the same time, this often leads to confusion, with the dog unsure whether to hold or drop his toy. Treat these as two separate tasks. Teach the leave using a tug toy so that you always remain in control. Play vigorously, then stop and command 'leave'. Keep the toy still and boring until he lets go, then click and treat.

5 Gradually build up how far your dog brings the toy, until he returns to you in one go. Once he can do this, add the command 'fetch'. Finally, teach your dog to keep hold of the toy until you take it. Once your dog brings the item to you, he may drop it when you click. Simply wait and don't treat. He is then likely to pick up the item – take it from him quietly and reward.

Key points

● Choose a retrieve item that is the right size, weight and material to suit your dog.

● If your dog is carrying the item, withhold the click to increase the distance he brings it – try to click before he drops it.

● If your dog drops the item before you have clicked him for carrying it, wait. He is likely to pick the item up again. You can then click and reward.

● Don't add the 'fetch' command until your dog understands the full task, otherwise it could come to mean chewing, mouthing or dropping the retrieve item.

Free time

Free time encourages your dog to think for himself, try different behaviours and work out how to get rewards. It builds confidence and curiosity, and improves his ability to learn and understand. You also learn a lot about him – what moves he favours and how smart he is.

1 Place your prop on the floor and sit down with a pot of treats. Your dog will soon learn that is his cue to do whatever he wants to earn rewards. Throw a treat into the basket to show this is what you are interested in. Now stay quiet and wait. Here, Gypsy jumps into the basket, so is clicked before she gets the treat.

2 We wait again to see what she does next. She stands up on the edge of the basket, so is clicked for that new behaviour and thrown a treat on the floor.

Key points

● With free time, maintain the momentum by keeping your dog moving – throw the treats in different directions.

● Don't 'zoom in' on a behaviour too quickly or your dog will become stuck and stop offering new moves.

● Reward anything to build your dog's confidence and creativity.

3 Next she stands with a paw on the basket handle. Again, she is clicked for a new behaviour and gets a treat.

4 Now she jumps in and lies down, so is clicked and given a treat. Continue to reward your dog for being creative by recognizing different behaviours.

5 'Zoom in' on a move you like by only rewarding that one, such as paws up on the handle. Click for both paws and add a command to cue the move.

Have a ball

Most dog's love ball tricks. Choose a ball that is light enough not to hurt your dog if it hits him, but strong enough for boisterous play. Make sure it is big enough not to be easily picked up in his mouth and held. If your dog already understands about using his nose to touch things (see page 158), he will find this trick easier. By teaching it as a nose trick, he will be less likely to mouth or bite the ball.

1 With your dog watching and in a wait, put a treat on the floor and place the ball on top of it.

2 Release your dog to get the treat, and as soon as his nose pushes the ball, click. Let him find his reward.

Key points

● If your dog doesn't nudge the ball straightaway when you stop placing a treat under it, simply wait. Be patient and don't worry about not 'telling' your dog what you want – a minute or two of thinking time is all that he needs.

● If your dog keeps biting at the ball, show him that using his nose is more rewarding. Click and reward only when he pushes it with his nose and withhold the click if he uses his teeth.

3 Repeat the sequence, placing treats under the ball in quick succession to build up momentum and encourage him to stand and move towards the ball.

Goal scoring

Once your dog understands this trick, why not add in a 'goal'? Stand close to your dog with your legs apart and command him to push the ball. Click and treat if he manages to put the ball through your legs. Practise this until he understands what you are asking for. You can then add a command 'shoot' and gradually build up the distance he needs to dribble the ball.

4 Once he gets the idea, leave out the treat. Click when he pushes the ball and throw a reward to keep him moving. When this is easy for him, add the command 'push'. Withhold the click until he has done two or three nudges and starts dribbling the ball.

Heading a ball

Once your dog can push a ball (see page 168), he will quickly learn how to 'head' it. For this trick to look slick, you have to throw the ball so that it is just above your dog's head to enable him to 'head' it. The better your throw, the more accurately he will return it.

1 Hold the ball out to your dog and give the command 'push' (see page 168). When he nudges the ball with his nose, click and treat. Repeat this several times so that your dog is confident about pushing the ball.

2 With your dog in 'sit, wait' (see page 44), step away. Keep the clicker in one hand and throw the ball so that it goes just above his head. As you throw, command 'push'.

Key points

● This trick just requires practice, practice and more practice to get reliable results.

● Don't overdo it in any one session, as a dog with a sore nose is not going to want to play.

● Don't be tempted to play tricks on your dog, such as suddenly using a heavier ball as this could destroy his confidence.

3 If he tries to nose the ball, click and treat. Practise to build his confidence and coordination. Soon he will start nosing the ball more purposefully and accurately – if not, practise Step 1 until he understands what you want.

4 Slowly extend the distance and the height that you throw the ball. As his 'headers' become more accurate you will be able to catch them. Click him only for the strikes that come back within your range.

On the ball

Before trying this trick, make sure your dog understands how to give both his front paws on command (see page 54). Also ensure that the ball is large and strong enough to suit your dog. If it is inflatable, check that it is firm so that it will not give when stood on. Choose a flat, level surface for this trick to enable the ball to move easily when your dog wishes it to, but not before.

1 Kneel down in front of your dog with the ball between you. Hold it steady and give your 'give paw' command (see page 54). As soon as he places a foot on the ball, click and treat. Repeat and then practise with the other paw in the same way.

2 Hold the ball and give your command for the left paw. When this is on the ball, do the same for the right paw. When both paws are on the ball, click and treat. Once he is confident with this, add the command 'on the ball' before you click and treat.

Key points

● Hold the ball still for your dog to start with to encourage his confidence. Don't be tempted to let it roll until your dog really has got the idea.

● Your dog is unlikely to be able to control the ball much to start with, so make sure there is nothing around that he could bump into.

3 When your dog will work from the verbal command, stand up. Continue to steady the ball with your foot.

4 Now try letting the ball roll. Take your foot off, and when your dog moves with the ball, click and treat. Repeat this several times. Gradually let the ball roll a little further before clicking and treating. Build this up until your dog can roll the ball himself.

Stepping up

This trick is an extension of the clock exercise used to teach your dog how to remain 'in front', whichever way you move (see page 92). Depending on what you have available for your dog to stand up on, you can develop this trick to become all four feet on the podium. Ideally, use something round so that your dog can easily circle it without having to stretch over corners. It also needs to be sturdy, steady and non-slip – a footstool is ideal.

1 Place a treat on the stool to indicate to your dog that this is what you are interested in. When his nose touches the stool, click and let him have the treat.

2 Now withhold the treat. Wait up to a minute to give your dog the opportunity to work out what else he can do to get a treat. A common response is to put a paw on the item. If he doesn't do this, encourage him by using the 'give paw' command (see page 54). As soon as a paw touches the stool, click and throw a treat. Repeat.

3 Now ask for both front paws on the stool. Either withhold the click once he has one paw up and wait for him to offer two, or when he has one foot in position, use your other 'give paw' command so that he brings the opposite foot up. When both paws are on the stool, click and throw a treat. Repeat. Once he has got the idea, add in the command 'on the stool' before clicking.

4 Now add the rotation by standing opposite
your dog. Face him and take a step around
the stool anticlockwise, commanding
'in front'. As your dog moves his hindlegs
to swing his hindquarters and remain facing
you, click and treat.

Key points

● Make sure your dog has already learned the 'in front' command on the floor (see page 92) before trying it on a stool.

● Practise rotating around the stool in both directions.

● This trick can be taught as 'free time' (see page 166) by using the stool as a prop. Click when your dog offers you paws on the stool and when he takes any steps.

● To develop this to four feet on the stool, withhold the click until your dog tries jumping up.

5 Take another step and repeat. You can then build up the number of steps taken at a time by withholding the click, until your dog can perform one or more full circles.

'Reading' your dog

Once you know the main clicker skills, you can teach tricks in a variety of ways. Successful training comes down to being able to 'read' your dog and present a task to him so that the correct response is the obvious one.

Time for bed

It is very handy to be able to send your dog to his bed and it's important that he is taught to do this in a positive way. He will learn that it is a good thing and associate it with reward. Teaching your dog to 'go to bed' is most easily done as an extended foot target exercise (see page 160). Use a blanket for his bed as the target marker.

1 Put your dog in a wait (see page 44) and the blanket on the floor a few steps in front of him. Stand on the opposite side of the blanket to your dog and place a treat on it just in front of you. Call your dog, and as soon as his feet (ideally all four) are on the blanket but before he gets the treat, click. Repeat several times.

2 Now repeat Step 1, but after your dog eats the treat, command him 'down' (see page 40). As soon as he lies on the blanket, click and treat again.

3 With your dog in a wait, place a treat on the furthest side of the blanket from your dog, but this time stand beside him. Release him and encourage him to get the treat. Click once his feet are on the blanket, but before he gets the treat. Repeat. Once he does this fluently, add the command 'on your bed'.

4 Now repeat Step 3 to send your dog to the blanket, telling him 'on your bed'. Then command your dog 'down' when he is on the blanket. Once he is lying down, click and treat. When your dog has got the idea, stop placing the treat on the blanket.

Transferable skills

In this task, the blanket becomes, in effect, a foot target and your dog learns that touching it results in rewards. Once he understands this, the item can be moved to different places and situations, but the task associated with it will stay the same – lie down and settle.

5 You can now place the blanket in your dog's usual bed, or in the car or wherever you wish him to settle down. With the command 'on your bed', he knows to go to that blanket wherever it is and chill out!

Key points

● Don't expect your dog necessarily to understand if you use a different blanket – a young or inexperienced dog will learn things in close connection to the context. An older dog may work it out easily. If in doubt, refresh your dog's memory of the task with the new bedding.

● Ask your dog to go a short way to his bed initially, until he understands the task. Once he has the idea, his bed may be in a different room or situation, and he will know to find it.

Get your skates on

If your dog has got the idea of foot targeting (see page 160), this is a straightforward trick to teach. The idea can then be applied to other objects, with the foot marker showing your dog where you want him to place his feet. Choose a skateboard that suits the size of your dog. Take time to teach this trick so that your dog is confident with the skateboard before you let it move.

1 Make sure your dog is confident with a foot target. Place it on a smooth floor and give the 'on your mark' command (see page 160). Click as soon as he touches the marker with both paws and throw the treat. Repeat several times.

2 Position the target on the skateboard so that the board won't tip up and frighten your dog. Hold the board still, command 'on your mark' and click and treat when his paws are on the target on the skateboard. Repeat several times.

Key points

● Throw the rewards for your dog so that he gets off the skateboard and has to return to it to earn another treat. This will make it easier to get the board to roll when he is ready.

● If your dog already understands 'on the ball' (see page 172) and 'on the stool' (see page 174), you can use the 'on the...' command to help him understand what you want more easily.

● Your dog is likely to favour one side for pushing. Bear this in mind for skateboarding.

3 Now remove the marker and see if your dog still places his paws on the skateboard. If he does transfer the behaviour, add the command 'skate', click and throw a treat. Practise this so that your dog understands the command. If he does not transfer the behaviour, do the exercise a few more times with the marker before trying again.

4 Now gradually introduce movement. Command him to 'skate', but do not steady the board. As he gets on, the skateboard will roll. Click and treat straight away. Gradually build up the distance by withholding the click.

Tidy up time

This trick is made up of a sequence of skills, each needing to be taught separately. Your dog has to be able to retrieve in order to pick up and drop items on command (see page 162). The different elements are linked by 'back-chaining'. You begin with the finish point of the task and build the sequence backwards, so your dog has to do a little more each time to reach the part of the trick he already knows well. The bin needs to be a little below his chin height and be large enough for your dog to put his head into easily. If your dog can't reach the bottom of the bin, put a false bottom in it. Choose 'rubbish' that your dog is happy to hold in his mouth. Here, scrunched up plain paper is used.

1 Position the bin close to you, between you and your dog. Place a treat in the bin and encourage your dog to get it. As he puts his head into the bin, but before he gets the treat, click. Let him eat the treat. Repeat several times to build his confidence with the prop.

Clicker clues

Teaching your dog tricks like putting rubbish in a bin is easy when you use the clicker to give him vital clues to the final goal – when you click you are saying 'yes, you're getting warmer'. When you do not click, you are telling him 'keep on trying and you'll get there in a minute'.

2 Place the 'rubbish' in the bin. Your dog is likely to investigate it – click once he noses it. Repeat a few times.

3 Now re-present the 'rubbish' in the bin, but don't click when he noses it – he will likely try to mouth or hold the paper. When he does, click. Try to click and treat while he still has his nose over the bin so that when he drops the paper to get his reward it falls back in. Repeat a few times.

4 Now place the 'rubbish' beside the bin and let your dog start to work out what you want. Click and treat when he noses or picks up the paper to begin with. Then withhold the click so that he has to try new things to get a reward. Click and treat for any action that will help shape the final task – for example, picking up the paper and taking a step towards the bin or simply putting his head in the bin again.

5 Gradually your dog will make the connection between being rewarded for putting his nose in the bin and for picking up the rubbish. When he places the paper in the bin, click and give a 'jackpot' of treats. Now practise and add the command 'in the bin'.

Key points

● Let your dog think the problem through – you may simply wait for up to a minute without giving a command or clicking, unless your dog does something that warrants a reward.

● Concentrate on helping your dog to make the link between the bin and the paper.

Shop, shop, shop!

This trick is quite complex – work on one bit at a time to avoid
overloading your dog. Before trying it, make sure he can retrieve
(see page 162), go to a target marker (see page 160) and perform the
wastebin trick (see page 184). Use a basket that has a broad base, to
prevent tipping, and a high handle so that it is easy for your dog to
get hold of, and get items in and out. Before starting to teach the full
trick, teach your dog to pick up the basket by its handle and to hold it.

1 With your dog in a wait (see page 44), place
the empty basket on your target mat a few
steps away. Send your dog to fetch the basket.
Click and reward once he has brought it to you.
Practise until fluent.

2 Ask him to hold the basket
and walk with him to the
target mat. Command him
to 'leave' (see page 164).
When he places it on the
mat, click and reward.

3 Send your dog, with the basket, to the mat with your target command. Once he is standing or sitting on the mat and holding the basket, click. Walk to him and reward. Practise, then try linking Steps 1–3 together.

4 Rehearse getting shopping into the basket using the same command and method as for the wastepaper trick. This time, place your 'shopping' next to the basket and only click and treat when he gets the items in the basket.

Key points

● It is better to teach all the basket tasks first, as these will be the least attractive to your dog. By teaching them first, you will have already attached a strong reward significance to them when you introduce the shopping items.

● The target mat will clarify to your dog where you want him to go and where to put the basket. In time, the mat can be removed.

5 Finally, teach him to carry the basket and 'shopping', first at heel and then by sending him to retrieve the full basket. Once he does this, try linking the whole sequence. Start by walking with your dog and work up to sending him to the mat and completing the other moves at a distance.

Index

Acknowledgements

With grateful thanks to Sue Evans, Avril James, Kay Laurence, Jan Morse, Gina Pink, and Beryl Rounsley.
Sports Connexion, Coventry CV8 3FL Tel 02476 306155

Executive Editor Trevor Davies
Editor Charles Hallam
Executive Art Director Mark Stevens
Designer Janis Utton
Special Photography © Octopus Publishing Group Limited /Angus Murray /Steve Gorton.
Other Photography © Octopus Publishing Group Limited /Angus Murray 7; Russell Sadur 19 bottom, 20; Steve Gorton 9; Tim Ridley 8.
Production Controller Manjit Sihra
Picture Researcher Taura Riley

Kizzy

Glen

Busy

Taz

Gypsy

Zoë

Mabel

Quincy

Rooney

Saffy

Keya

Foxy

Chester

Bailey